10-Minute Cuisine

10-Minute Cuisine

10-Minute
CUISINE

HENRIETTA GREEN AND
MARIE-PIERRE MOINE

Conran Octopus

DEDICATION

To Auden of Portobello and Dickie
of Amboise – our faithful friends

Throughout the book the half-plate
symbol ◑ has been used to
indicate a starter portion, and the
full-plate symbol ● to denote a
main-course portion. Recipes are
for 4 people, unless otherwise
stated.

Editorial Direction: Lewis Esson
Publishing
Design: Paul Welti
Photography: Jess Koppel
Illustration: David Downton
Food for Photography: Meg Jansz
Styling: Penny Mishcon
Editorial Assistant: Penny David
Production: Sonya Sibbons

First published in 1991 by
Conran Octopus Limited
37 Shelton Street, London WC2H 9HN

This paperback edition published in 1992 by
Conran Octopus Limited

Text copyright (c) Henrietta Green &
Marie-Pierre Moine 1991

British Library Cataloguing in
Publication data
Moine, Marie-Pierre
Ten minute cuisine.
A. Cookery
I. Title I]. Green, Henrietta
641.555

ISBN 1-85029-449-6

Typeset by Servis Filmsetting Limited
Printed and bound by Kim Hup Lee Printing
Co PTE Ltd, Singapore

Contents

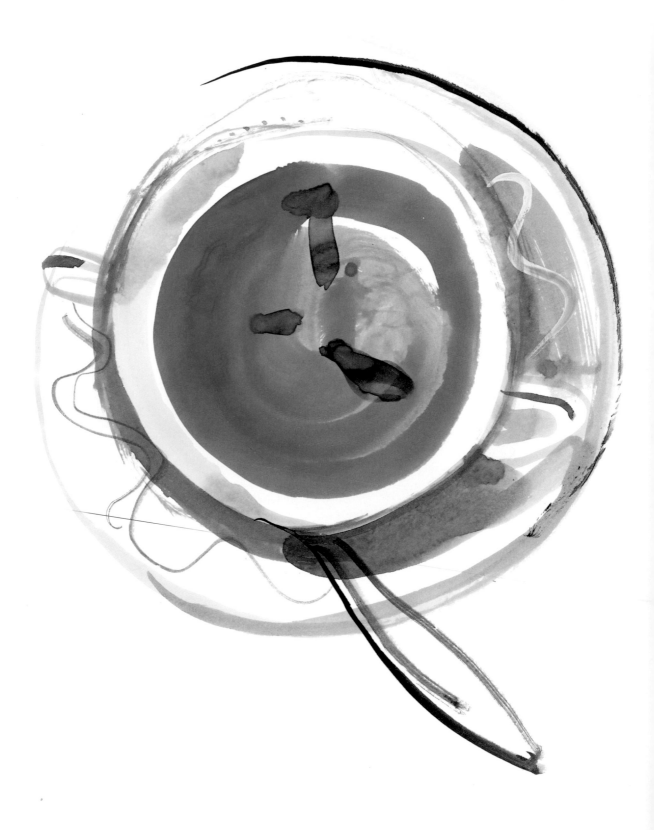

Introduction

10-minute Cuisine *is the result of our love of good food and lack of time to prepare it. We have written the book for everyone who, like us, can cook and enjoys doing so but has neither the time – nor, perhaps, the inclination – to spend a lot of time in the kitchen.*

We had real problems in the past, as we liked to eat fresh food but were both very busy. We tried microwave cooking and found that, as a basic way of cooking, it just was not for us. We then tried cooked-chilled food and, frankly, the dishes were boring, over-priced, under-seasoned and laden with preservatives. In desperation, we evolved our own ways of cooking good fresh food very fast.

We turned ourselves into cooks 'à la 10-minute' – the domestic equivalent of short-order cooks. In our case, the back-up brigade consisted of the right ingredients, the right techniques and the right equipment – including a food processor, which has proved invaluable!

In 10 minutes there is only so much you can achieve. Subtlety is out; but intense flavours,

clean sharp tastes and firm textures more than make up for it. The idea is to turn the lack of time to an advantage.

If you think this sounds daunting and involves too much frantic activity, you could not be more wrong. 10-minute cuisine is fun, brisk and enjoyable. The secret lies in concentrating on quality produce; preparing it quickly and effectively; and in using the most suitable equipment. We have cut out all unnecessary details – from fiddly preparations to fancy garnishes – and pared the process down to the essentials.

We may be mean with our time but we are certainly liberal with our food: a generous table needs no trimmings. We do not go for elaborate presentation or individual plating – everyone helps themselves straight from the pot and from large bowls and dishes.

10-minute Cuisine *means the busiest person can enjoy cooking – and even entertaining! We love our fast food: it is bold, vibrant and gutsy; and the dishes are full of flavour and freshness. We hope you will have as much fun cooking and eating it as we do.*

Ingredients

10-minute cuisine is bold, decisive and very quick. Our fast approach relies essentially on the quality of the ingredients we use and is unlike most traditional methods of cooking, where flavours are gently nursed and coaxed until they are developed to the full.

Since we have no time for long braises or slow simmers, what we are aiming for is the fastest possible release of the taste of ingredients. For this reason we always use the best – the freshest and most intensely flavoured – produce.

Obviously, this great burst of taste can only be achieved if the ingredients are good enough to start with. First of all they must be fresh. Consequently we are great believers in the old-fashioned way of shopping 'little and often', so that the food we use never sits around for long. This practice includes staples such as eggs, butter, cheese and the spices in our store cupboard, as well as the more obvious vegetables, fruit, meat and fish. Everything must be in top condition.

We also try to buy produce in season. Not only is it better value, but very often it is at its peak of flavour as it has ripened at its natural pace. What we save on buying seasonally, we may spend on convenience. This sometimes takes the form of pre-washed and cut vegetables, pre-packed and selected salad leaves, boned and trimmed meat or skinned and filleted fish. They cost more, but they do save precious time.

One of our many extravagances – for which we offer no apology – is the liberal use of fresh herbs. With their pungent flavours, they are invaluable for fast and bold cooking and are far more effective than dried herbs. We also use extra-virgin olive oil – not just for dressings, but also for cooking – and we assume you will too. The wine we cook with is the wine we drink. So-called 'cooking' wines can spoil the flavour of a sauce. You will find that in many of our recipes we do not specify which wine to use – but we do assume that it will be on the dry side.

We do, however, specify wine vinegar or cider vinegar, as – in our opinion – their contribution is unique. Any other vinegars – malt in particular – are so sharp that they could destroy the dish. Both of us only ever use sea salt, because you need less of it and it blends better with – and brings out more rapidly – the flavour of the food. For the same reasons we only ever use freshly ground black pepper.

In an ideal world we would buy only organic produce, as the flavour is usually stronger. Unfortunately, the price is often prohibitive so we have to compromise. One thing we insist on is unwaxed citrus fruit, particularly if we are using the zest. 'Waxing' is a euphemism for coating fruit with a nasty cocktail of chemicals, particularly anti-fungal preparations (which stop the fruit from getting mouldy but are neither healthy nor flavoursome). If you have to use waxed fruit, scrub the skin with a stiff brush several times in warm soapy water, rinse well and pat dry.

On the vexed question of eggs, as we occasionally use lightly cooked – or even raw – eggs, we try to buy them from trusted sources which guarantee them to be safe.

In fact, we generally try to buy from smaller speciality producers or specialist shops which assure us of good service, personal attention and the freshness and quality of their produce. This makes shopping much more satisfying. If you are tempted to pursue our style of cooking, perhaps you too should build up your own network of suppliers.

Since, more often than not, the occasions on which you have to cook in 10 minutes are precisely those when you are most pushed for time, it helps to keep a few basics in the kitchen. Obviously we always have staples such as:

IN THE LARDER:

EGGS
BUTTER
GARLIC
SEA SALT
BLACK PEPPERCORNS
SUGAR

which get turned over pretty quickly. Although we have already said we prefer to buy food when and if we need it, we list below items which will keep for a while and are frequently very useful:

IN THE REFRIGERATOR:

MILK
2 OR 3 LEMONS AND ORANGES
BUNCH OF SPRING ONIONS
BOTTLE OF DRY WHITE WINE
SOME RASHERS OF BACON
LARGE CARTON OF YOGHURT
CHUNK OF PARMESAN
DRY CIDER

IN THE FREEZER:

PACKET OF BUTTER
CHICKEN/ VEGETABLE/ FISH
  STOCK (EITHER HOME-MADE,
  WHEN WE ARE LESS PUSHED
  FOR TIME, OR BOUGHT)
TUB OF GOOD QUALITY VANILLA
  ICE-CREAM
PACKET OF LEAF SPINACH
PACKET OF SMALL GARDEN
  PEAS
LOAF OF GOOD BREAD

ON THE WINDOW SILL:

Since we do use such a lot of different fresh herbs, we try to grow as many as we can on our window sills. Not only does this save money, time and effort; but it is also great fun.

Most big supermarket chains now sell plastic containers of growing herbs: parsley, coriander, chives, thyme, basil, chervil, sage, tarragon and mint. These cost no more than a tiny packet of cut fresh herbs, but they last much longer and we highly recommend them.

We make an exception for flat-leaf parsley, which we prefer to the moss-curled variety. As we are constantly using it in vast quantities, we buy it in bunches. These we keep in the kitchen: either in a jug of water on a shady window ledge or in the refrigerator, wrapped in damp newspaper inside a polythene bag.

IN THE STORE CUPBOARD:

10-MINUTE RICE

DRIED PASTA AND/OR NOODLES

EXTRA-VIRGIN OLIVE OIL

GROUNDNUT OR SUNFLOWER OIL

WALNUT OIL AND/OR HAZELNUT
  OIL

RED AND WHITE WINE VINEGAR

CIDER VINEGAR

½ BOTTLE OF DRY SHERRY

SOY SAUCE

MUSTARD POWDER

WORCESTERSHIRE SAUCE

GOOD MUSTARD (KEEP IN
  REFRIGERATOR ONCE
  OPENED)

ANCHOVY FILLETS

ANCHOVY ESSENCE

TAHINI

TABASCO

HARISSA OR CHILLI SAUCE

CORIANDER SEEDS

NUTMEG

PAPRIKA

CUMIN

SMALL DRIED CHILLIS

CAPERS

HONEY

REDCURRANT JELLY

MARMALADE

BLANCHED ALMONDS

SEEDLESS RAISINS

PINE NUTS/HAZELNUTS/
  WALNUTS

POPPY SEEDS/SUNFLOWER
  SEEDS

STORE SAUCES (SEE PAGE 18)

TINS (SEE PAGE 20)

INGREDIENTS

STORE-CUPBOARD SAUCES

The 10-minute cook can prepare these invaluable sauces when there is time, then store and use them later to give added interest and extra flavour to a wide variety of dishes. We usually have at least a couple on the go at any one time. They are a boon when there is no time for shopping or an unexpected meal to cook: they are great for perking up anything from pasta to a pudding, and can be used to make a quick paste-paint or even a savoury butter.

1 SUN-DRIED TOMATOES IN OIL

You can buy sun-dried tomatoes in oil, but they are expensive and a little bland. We prefer to buy them dried, and bottle them in oil ourselves. We are indebted to Anna Del Conte, whose recipe from *Secrets from an Italian Kitchen* produces a particularly deep and pungent flavour.

Cover 450g/1lb sun-dried tomatoes with a mixture of equal parts boiling water and wine vinegar and leave them to soak for 1 hour. Turn them over and leave them for a further 1½ hours. Drain and pat dry with kitchen paper.

In a clean glass jar, place the tomatoes in layers, sprinkling each layer with handfuls of snipped oregano and chopped garlic. Pour in extra-virgin olive oil to cover (about 300ml/½pt), making sure there is no air trapped between the layers by sliding a palette knife down the side of the jar. Leave to steep until required.

2 LABNA BALLS IN OIL

Again, you can buy labna balls in oil from Greek and Turkish delicatessens. However, we generally prefer the flavour of home-made ones. The method we use comes from Peter Graham's *Classic Cheese Cookery*, but the flavourings are our own.

Pour 2 large (300ml/½pt) cartons of Greek-style strained cows' milk yoghurt into a colander lined with several layers of damp muslin. Leave this to stand in a bowl overnight in a cool place.

Next day, tie the muslin into a bundle and suspend this over the bowl for about another 24 hours to extract more whey and to make the labna even firmer.

Untie the muslin and roll the labna a little at a time into small balls, about 4cm/1½in diameter, between the palms of your hands. Place the balls in layers in a clean glass jar, sprinkling each layer with equal parts of a mixture of the zest of 1 orange and 1 lemon, 1 snipped spring onion, a handful of snipped flat-leaf parsley and 2 crushed black peppercorns. Pour in 1 tablespoon of orange flower water and then cover with extra-virgin olive oil.

3 CHILLI OIL

We find flavoured oils extremely useful when cooking in 10 minutes. There are endless variations, but because of our approach we go for strong flavours with plenty of punch – Chilli Oil is one of the most versatile.

To prepare it, simply take a handful of small chilli peppers (remember – the thinner the chilli, the hotter it is), prick them all several times with a needle and put them in a clean jar covered with extra-virgin olive oil. Leave to steep for at least 1 week.

It is less fiery than most commercial chilli oils, but still use it sparingly!

4 ROASTED GARLIC IN OIL

Heat the oven to 180C/350F/gas4. Paint 3 heads of garlic lightly with olive oil and sprinkle them with sea salt. Bake them on a tray in the oven for 45 minutes. Leave to cool, then put them in a clean jar and pour in enough extra-virgin olive oil to cover.

To use: break off as many cloves as you need, and squeeze them to extract the pulp.

5 TAPENADE

Stone 170g/6oz black olives. In the food processor, whizz them along with 3 garlic cloves, a handful of mixed thyme, rosemary and oregano, a dash each of Tabasco and anchovy essence and a pinch of ground coriander. Trickle in 6 tablespoons of extra-virgin olive oil and whizz again. Spoon into a clean bowl or jar, cover and chill until needed. Tapenade will keep for up to 1 month in the refrigerator.

6 PRUNES IN BRANDY

Take 450g/1lb large prunes and pack them loosely into a clean glass jar. Break up a small stick of cinnamon, add the pieces to the jar along with the zest of 1 orange. Make a light syrup by boiling 170g/6oz sugar with 150ml/$\frac{1}{4}$pt water for 5 minutes. Leave to cool and pour into the jar. Top up with brandy, seal the jar and give it a thorough shake. Leave for at least 1 week.

7 RAISINS IN WHISKY

Take 225g/8oz seedless raisins and pack them loosely in a clean glass jar. Pour in enough whisky to cover and leave to soak for 1 or 2 days. Top up with extra whisky if required.

12 THINGS TO DO WITH TINS

All our recipes are based on fresh ingredients because that is how we like to cook. However, quite a few good things can come out of tins. Here are our 'Top 12', and we suggest that you always have some of the following tins in stock.

CLAMS (IN BRINE)

TUNA (IN OIL)

ARTICHOKE HEARTS

CANNELLINI BEANS

CHICKPEAS

FLAGEOLETS

PETIT POIS

SWEETCORN

SWEET RED PEPPERS

TOMATOES

CHESTNUT PURÉE
  (SWEETENED)

BLACK CHERRIES (IN SYRUP)

1 SWEETCORN SOUP

Tip the contents of a large tin of sweetcorn into a saucepan. Half fill the tin with water and top up the rest with milk. Pour this into the pan, add a dash of white wine and a few sprigs of thyme and bring to a simmer. Stir in 1 or 2 tablespoons of single cream and season to taste with sea salt and freshly ground black pepper.

2 ARTICHOKE AND BLACK OLIVE SAUCE

Drain the contents of a medium tin of artichoke hearts. Roughly chop the hearts and put them in a bowl. Snip in some parsley and stoned black olives and stir in a little olive oil. Season with sea salt and freshly ground black pepper. Mix into cooked and drained pasta (see No-cook Sauces for Pasta on page 45).

3 RED PEPPER AND TUNA SAUCE

Drain the contents of a medium tin of sweet red peppers and a small tin of tuna. Roughly chop the peppers and mix with the tuna. Snip in some chives and stir in a little olive oil. Season with sea salt and freshly ground black pepper. Mix into cooked and drained pasta (see No-cook Sauces for Pasta on page 45).

4 CLAM AND TOMATO SAUCE

Bring to the boil the contents of a medium tin of tomatoes with a crushed garlic clove, a pinch of sugar and some snipped oregano and thyme. Simmer for 3 minutes until slightly thickened. Add a dash each of white wine and olive oil and simmer for another 1 minute. Drain the contents of a small tin of clams and tip the clams into the sauce. Stir gently until heated through and season to taste with sea salt and freshly ground black pepper. This is an ideal hot pasta sauce (see pages 44-7).

5 PEA AND CREAM SAUCE

Drain the contents of a medium tin of petits pois. Tip the peas into a saucepan along with a small carton (150ml/¼pt) of single cream and bring to a simmer. Season to taste with sea salt and freshly ground black pepper. Pour over cooked and drained pasta (see pages 44–7). Snip over a few lettuce leaves.

6 INSTANT HUMMUS

Whizz together the drained contents of a medium tin of chickpeas, a couple of garlic cloves, some olive oil, a little tahini and the juice of ½ a lemon. Season to taste with sea salt and freshly ground black pepper. Sprinkle with a little paprika, snip over some coriander. Serve with black olives.

7 BEAN AND TUNA SALAD

Drain and rinse the contents of a medium tin of cannellini beans and drain a small tin of tuna. Mix them together, snip over 1 or 2 spring onions and some parsley. Stir in a little olive oil, the juice of ½ a lemon and season to taste with sea salt and freshly ground black pepper.

8 CHICKPEA AND TAHINI SALAD

Drain and rinse the contents of a medium tin of chickpeas. Stir in a little tahini, a dash of wine vinegar, a couple of chopped tomatoes and snip over some mint. Season to taste with sea salt and freshly ground black pepper.

9 RED PEPPER SAUCE

Whizz the drained contents of a small tin of sweet red peppers with a garlic clove and a little olive oil. Season to taste with sea salt and freshly ground black pepper. Ideal with grilled chicken or hamburgers.

10 FLAGEOLETS

Drain and rinse the contents of a medium tin of flageolets. Melt a knob of butter in a sauté pan and add the flageolets. Snip in a couple of spring onions and add a dash of white wine. Heat through gently and season to taste with sea salt and freshly ground black pepper. Ideal with grilled lamb cutlets.

11 CHESTNUT PURÉE WITH YOGHURT

Whizz the contents of a small tin of chestnut purée with a large carton (300ml/½pt) of thick set yoghurt, the zest and juice of ½ an orange and a dash of brandy. Sweeten to taste with honey or sugar.

12 CHERRY SAUCE

Tip the contents of a small tin of black cherries into a saucepan. Add a generous dash of Kirsch and heat gently. Ideal with ice-cream.

Equipment

There is no getting around the fact that in order to cook fresh food very fast, you need to have a relatively well-equipped kitchen and, to save time, the right appliances for the job. We are assuming that the reader already has a basic batterie de cuisine, *which includes a few good quality utensils and gadgets such as a sieve, a colander, a couple of whisks, various wooden spoons and a couple of spatulas.*

What we do not intend is that anyone spend money on unnecessary high-tech clutter, or the latest multi-function microwave. In fact, one of us does not even own a microwave and the other only uses it to re-heat coffee.

However, there is one major piece of equipment we feel is worth investing in, and that is a food processor. We are addicted to our food processors, because they do everything very fast and very efficiently. We both own a Magimix Système Cuisine 3000, which has an additional smaller bowl for small quantities of sauces and purées. We have found that the more boldly and frequently you use a food processor, the more satisfactory the results. Without them, frankly, we could never even have contemplated writing this book, as most of the recipes would have taken three times as long.

A number of other tools are essential for our 10-minute cuisine. These are as follows:

UTENSILS & GADGETS

KNIVES

Good knives are invaluable, as our approach to cooking involves fast preparation as much as fast cooking. We suggest you use whatever shape and size of knife you are most comfortable with. It goes without saying that you must keep your knives sharp and within easy reach.

ZESTER

You will need a zester for zesting fruit (see page 31). This is a useful little utensil with tiny holes at the end of its blade which shave off thin strips of peel without lifting off any of the bitter pith just underneath. It is a boon when every second counts and you have no time to blanch the peel.

SCISSORS

Scissors are important as we use them for snipping (see page 30). There are a number of specialist kitchen scissors available – from fish scissors to poultry shears – but we are more than happy with the all-purpose ones providing you keep them very sharp. For reasons of hygiene, you really ought to have at least 3 pairs: one for herbs and vegetables; one for cooked meat and fish; and a third strictly reserved for raw meat and fish. A good idea is to buy each pair with a different colour handle and this, in turn, could be colour-coordinated with one of 3 corresponding chopping boards.

BRUSH

For paste-painting (see page 31) a brush is essential. Choose a strong well-made brush which can cope with applying a heavy paste without bending or shedding bristles. Whether it is flat or round is immaterial, but if there is a large surface to paint, a wide brush will obviously do the job much quicker. Nylon bristles are fine, but bear in mind that they may melt when used on a hot surface.

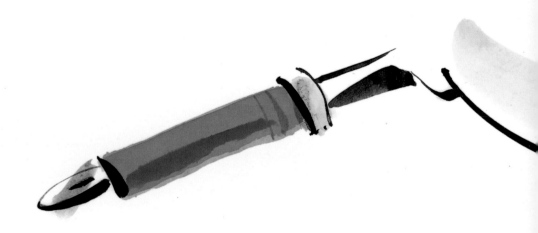

SALAD SPINNER

When it comes to washing salads, time can be saved by using a salad spinner. This relatively inexpensive gadget is a sophisticated version of the old-fashioned salad shaker and utilizes the principle of centrifugal force. The washed leaves are put in an inner rotating basket and as it spins, the water is driven out to the outer bowl. For the few pounds they cost, we think they are an excellent investment.

WOK & SCOOP

Since we stir-fry a lot (see page 32), a wok and wok scoop are important. Our woks are the 'cheap and cheerful' variety acquired at the nearest Chinese supermarket and are replaced relatively frequently as they quickly rust or discolour. As neither of us is particularly skilled or strong-wristed, we prefer the classic single-handled model which is far easier to manipulate.

SAUTÉ PAN

A good sauté pan is incredibly versatile. With its deep sides, it is more flexible than a frying pan and we use it to sauté, steam-boil (see page 32) and poach – all vital methods for cooking fresh food fast. We recommend investing in a good-quality heavy-based pan, made from copper or teflon (or any other non-stick material). As we use our sauté pan for steam-boiling, it should also have a tight-fitting lid.

For sautéing small amounts of food, and also for cooking Eggahs (see page 51), we use a 17cm/7in copper-based omelette pan.

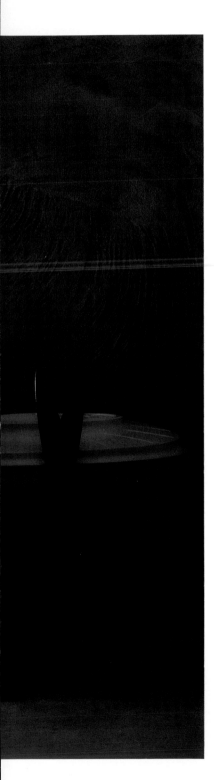

PASTA PAN

We cook a lot of pasta and have both bought a proper pasta pan – ruinously expensive, but an investment we have never regretted. A pasta pan is made from stainless steel, and is deep-sided with a fitted draining basket and a tight-fitting lid. To drain the cooked pasta, all you do is lift out the basket.

APPLIANCES

An efficient hob is essential. We are happier with gas because the heat is instant and easier to control.

Obviously every kitchen has an oven, but we hardly ever use ours for fast cooking as – whether gas or electric – it takes too long to heat up. However, as grilling is one of our basic techniques (see page 31), a good grill is also required. We both have oven grills which work perfectly provided we remember to heat them up for a few minutes in advance. Lining the grill pan with foil not only makes it easier to clean but also speeds up grilling, as it reflects the heat.

Should you not have a built-in grill, the alternatives are a grill pan, a griddle, a built-in barbecue or an infra-red electric grill.

A grill pan is usually made of ridged cast iron. Before use it is lightly brushed with oil to prevent the food from sticking, then it is heated on the hob. The surface of the food is instantly seared on contact with the hot grill pan, which is particularly good for red meat or a whole fish.

A griddle is also heated on top of the hob. Usually made from a thinner layer of cast iron, it has a flat surface and is more suitable for cooking vegetables.

The built-in electric barbecue is a great luxury but, if you can afford it, a delight to cook with. There are various models on the market which all work on the same principle: a steel container, holding lava rocks and a heating element, is set into a work surface. Once the rocks are hot, the food can be grilled either directly on them or over removable steel grids.

An infra-red electric grill is free-standing and produces a higher temperature than most built-in oven grills.

Techniques

10-minute Cuisine is all about preparing and cooking food very fast. In such a short time we could not be expected to use subtle or complex techniques. Very often we find that the quickest way to mix, tear or break ingredients is to use our hands. We have evolved a number of straightforward methods which do the job with minimum fuss but maximum effect. Like our whole approach to cooking, they take no time at all to master.

WHIZZING

This is a word you will find in most of our recipes. What it means is to process food just long enough in a food processor to achieve a desired texture. The timing will vary depending on whether the item is to be roughly chopped or smoothly puréed.

To whizz efficiently, first break, slice or snip the food into manageable pieces (the exact size will obviously be dictated by the texture, but generally never more than 7.5cm/3in).

Whizzing is done with the basic knife blade. If a recipe requires grated, shredded or sliced ingredients, we specify which other disc or blade to use.

SLICING

There is nothing complicated about the way we slice ingredients. Our aim is to produce food with as much flavour and texture as possible and, as we have to achieve this in 10 minutes, both preparation and cooking are as speedy as possible. Since every minute counts, there is a danger that fastidious slicing may become counter-productive and take up too much time.

Often we find that precise slicing, measuring and weighing are unnecessary and waste vital seconds – we prefer instead to go by appearance. For example, when cooking meat, fish fillets or boned poultry breasts very fast they will probably need to be sliced either in half lengthwise or into long thin strips.

A word of warning! Do not cut too finely: there is always the possibility that the pieces may collapse into a unappetizing pulp.

Vegetables can be sliced either with a knife or in the food processor. The method to use depends on quantity and personal preference. Frankly, unless large quantities are being prepared, it is often not worth dirtying the food processor.

SLIVERING & SHREDDING

Particularly for stir-frying, vegetables can also be slivered or shredded. To sliver, just cut them across at a sharp angle into pieces no wider than 1cm/½in.

Shredding can be done with the hands or by thinly slicing bunched-up food: particularly lettuce, cabbage or spinach leaves; and ham or boned chicken breasts.

SNIPPING

Perhaps we use our scissors more than most, but we think the quickest way to prepare herbs, bacon rashers, ham, spring onions, anchovy fillets – and sometimes even fish – is to snip them.

Snipping has many advantages: it is incredibly fast; it saves on washing up, as you can snip directly over – or into – a pan or dish; and it is labour-saving as it allows whole handfuls to be cut in one go.

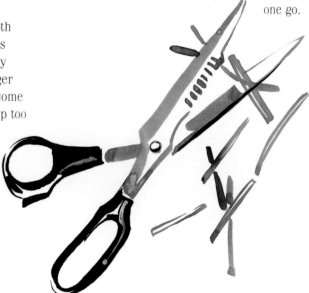

ZESTING

As there is no time for marinating or slow simmers, we find that adding the zest of citrus fruit is a marvellous way of intensifying flavour and adding texture.

Of course zest should really be blanched (to tenderize and remove any bitterness), but we just do not have the time. For our purposes the best zest is the thinnest, with as little pith as possible. So when using a zester, try not to press it down too firmly against the fruit as this also brings up a thick layer of white and bitter pith.

PASTE-PAINTING

In 10-minute cuisine, paste-painting is the alternative to marinating. The secret to successful paste-painting lies in the paste – this must be strong-flavoured, full-bodied and thick-textured.

What the paste does while the food is cooking is to create a coating which seals in the flavour (both its own and that of the coated item) and adds to the taste and texture. The technique is fun and simple to use, and works best of all when grilling. Simply paint the paste evenly all over the food.

GRILLING

Everybody is familiar with grilling. All we want to add, when it comes to 10-minute cooking, is that the heat – whether applied from above or below – should be very hot and the food thinly sliced. (Particularly if you have an electric grill, use any preparation time to get the grill good and hot before you cook!)

SEARING

Searing, sometimes called 'seizing', is very fast grilling or pan-frying in order to seal in juices and flavour. Seared food is often paste-painted first and the technique works particularly well with the firm strong flesh of red meat or salmon.

SAUTÉING OR PAN-FRYING

Again, this is a basic technique used by everybody. For our purposes, we first slice, snip, shred or sliver the food into small pieces. Then, while sautéing, we keep the heat moderate to prevent the food from burning. This method means that you can finish off the dish by making a quick sauce conveniently in the same pan.

STIR-FRYING

The Chinese are masters of this technique. It is an excellent way of cooking fresh food very fast and is ideal for 10-minute cooking. The food must be cut, sliced or snipped into small pieces for successful stir-frying.

A wok – with its deep sides and rounded bottom – is essential. First oil or grease it lightly, then put it over a high heat. Once the food is added to the wok, use a wok scoop to keep it on the move – this also applies to Stir-fried Eggs (see page 50). The shape of the wok enables cooked food to be pushed up the sides while more ingredients are being put in the pan to be cooked. Obviously, always start with whatever takes longest to cook. Extra liquid is sometimes added for later simmering.

BLANCHING

This simply means plunging food – in our case, only vegetables – in boiling water for a minute or two to soften them slightly. They must then be refreshed quickly in cold water to stop the cooking and keep their colour.

POACHING

Poaching is a gentle method of cooking which lends itself well to fish and poultry. Use a well-flavoured poaching liquid – such as a good stock, wine or fruit juice – and bring it to a simmer. Keep it bubbling very gently over a low-to-moderate heat and bear in mind that the food is likely to toughen if the liquid is actually allowed to boil.

STEAM-BOILING

Much as we like conventional steaming, there is no time for it in 10-minute cuisine. The best alternative is steam-boiling. As you would expect, this method is a cross between boiling and steaming, using a minimum amount of liquid in a pan with a tight-fitting lid over a high heat. Steam-boiling is a very efficient way of cooking vegetables (see page 104).

REDUCING

In conventional cooking, reduction is the slow process of boiling down a liquid to intensify its flavour and, very often, thicken its texture. In our terminology, all it means is that we turn up the heat a little and boil vigorously in an uncovered pan to generate maximum flavour in as short a time as possible.

FINISHING OR DEGLAZING

Finishing is an easy way of 'deglazing' a pan to make a quick sauce. Once the food is cooked, remove it from the pan and keep it warm. Then add a little liquid, such as stock, wine, vinegar, cream – or even a knob of butter – to the cooking juices in the pan. Next turn up the heat and, using a wooden spoon, scrape and stir the sediment in the pan until the juices thicken to a sauce-like consistency. Then simply spoon this over the food.

WARMING PLATES

The way we cook does not allow for fancy presentation or trimmings, which is why we never individually plate food. Instead, we arrange it on a serving dish from which everyone may help themselves. We always try to warm the dish and, where appropriate, will try also to warm the plates. There are several quick ways of ensuring that the dishes and plates are warm:
1) Hold or place them under hot running water for a minute or two and then leave them to drain.
2) Pour the contents of a hot kettle over them and then leave them to drain.
3) Place them, one at a time, under a hot grill for a second or two.
4) Where a safe fit allows, perch them on the tops of saucepans.

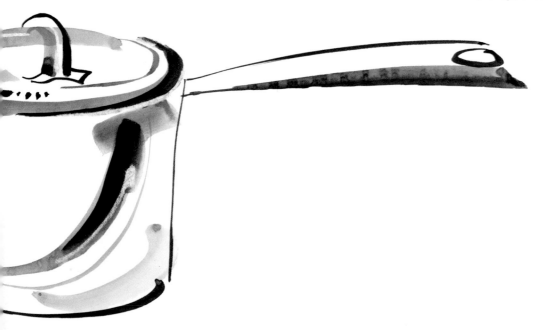

Soups

Soups are an integral part of our '10-minute' approach, whether served as a starter or as main course.

Contrary to popular belief there is no need to simmer a soup for hours – providing you start with fresh ingredients, full of flavour, which are then finely sliced, snipped or zested.

We are not great fans of stock cubes – as we have yet to find one that does a better job than water and sea salt; however, stock is needed to cook some of these soups. Use either home-made (if you have the time and inclination) or look out for the finely balanced fresh stocks that are sold chilled in cartons. Relatively new on supermarket shelves, they are as good as the real thing and, since they are still quite hard to find, we suggest stocking up your freezer with them when you find a supply.

As a guide to quantity we find that 1.1 litres/2pints of soup is about the right amount for 4 people.

Avocado, Spinach and Lemon Soup (page 36)

NO-COOK SOUPS

Our 'no-cook' cold soups really can be made in minutes and are breathtakingly simple – as long as you have a food processor!

To speed the process even further, we do not peel the vegetables – just give them a thorough wash and chop them roughly into pieces of a size the food processor can easily handle.

To keep no-cook soups as fresh-tasting as possible it is best to make them at the last minute. If you like them chilled, add a few ice cubes to the mixture while whizzing it in the processor, or float a couple in each serving bowl.

1 PINE KERNEL SOUP

Process a handful of pine kernels and a clove of garlic to a smooth paste. Add a couple of slices of wholemeal bread (crusts removed) and an egg, then process again. Slowly pour in 300ml/½pt olive oil followed by 300ml/½pt water and whizz to a smooth paste. Pour in 3 tablespoons of sherry vinegar and season to taste with sea salt and freshly ground black pepper. If the soup is too solid, add a little more water or some ice and whizz again.

2 AVOCADO, SPINACH AND LEMON SOUP

Process 450g/1lb trimmed baby spinach leaves, then add a couple of roughly chopped ripe avocados and the juice of 1 lemon. Whizz until smooth, adding about 700ml/1¼pt water or stock until the soup is the right consistency. Season to taste with Tabasco, sea salt and freshly ground black pepper.

3 CUCUMBER AND TARRAGON SOUP

Peel, halve lengthwise and scrape out the pips of a large cucumber. Process with a handful of fresh tarragon and a large (300ml/½pt) carton of yoghurt. Season to taste with sea salt and freshly ground black pepper.

4 TOMATO SOUP

Roughly chop 450g/1lb ripe tomatoes. Whizz until fluffy and airy. Season to taste with sea salt, freshly ground black pepper and a dash of sugar, if the tomatoes are not very sweet. Serve garnished with some fresh basil leaves.

5 MELON SOUP

Quarter 2 ripe melons, scrape out the pips and scoop out the flesh. Process the flesh with 1 tablespoon honey, a handful of mint leaves, the juice of 1 lemon and a small carton (150ml/¼pt) of sheep's milk yoghurt. Season to taste with sea salt and freshly ground black pepper.

6 TARATOR

Peel, halve lengthwise and scrape out the pips of a large cucumber. Process with a handful of walnuts, a couple of garlic cloves, some fresh parsley, 2 tablespoons of olive oil and a large (300ml/½pt) carton of yoghurt. If the soup is too solid, add ice cubes and whizz again. Season to taste.

HOT SOUPS

Edouard de Pomiane, the celebrated French gastronome of the 1930s and great master of the art of cooking in 10 minutes, had 'an invariable rite'. No matter what he was cooking, the first thing he did was to bring to the boil plenty of water.

For hot soups this certainly applies, although for some recipes it may be stock, or wine and water, which should be heated.

HERB VELOUTÉ

1.1L/2PT WATER
SMALL BUNCHES OF FRESH
   HERBS, INCLUDING: PARSLEY,
   WATERCRESS, CHERVIL AND
   TARRAGON
100ML/4FLOZ SOUR CREAM
SEA SALT AND FRESHLY GROUND
   BLACK PEPPER
BUTTER, TO FINISH

1   Bring the water to the boil.

2   Snip the herbs into 250ml/½pt boiling water and simmer for 5 minutes.

3   Process to a smooth texture. Whizz in the cream.

4   Return to the pan, add the rest of the water. Season to taste and serve with a knob of butter on top of each plate of soup.

LETTUCE AND PEA SOUP

1.1L/2PT WATER
2 RASHERS OF RINDLESS
   SMOKED BACON
2 SPRING ONIONS
225G/8OZ FROZEN PEAS
1 COS LETTUCE (OR 2 LITTLE
   GEMS)
FEW LEAVES OF SUMMER
   SAVORY (OR SPRIGS OF
   THYME)
150ML/¼PT SINGLE CREAM
SEA SALT AND FRESHLY GROUND
   BLACK PEPPER

1   Bring the water to the boil in a kettle.

2   Heat a large saucepan, snip in the bacon and dry-fry for 1 minute.

3   Snip in the spring onions and cook until they are just softened.

4   Add the peas and cover with boiling water. Stir and simmer for 2 minutes.

5   Snip in the lettuce and summer savory. Simmer for a further 3 minutes.

6   Process to a smooth texture. Whizz in the cream. Return to the pan, pour in the rest of the hot water and season to taste.

CARROT AND ORANGE SOUP

Use young baby carrots as they seldom need scraping, need hardly any cooking and taste far fresher and sweeter than older woody varieties.

For extra depth of colour use a blood orange. Whatever you do, do not let the soup come to the boil as this will ruin the flavour.

450G/1LB YOUNG CARROTS
1.1L/2PT WATER OR STOCK
25G/1OZ BUTTER
3 SPRING ONIONS
1 TBSP GROUND CUMIN
1 ORANGE
100ML/4FLOZ DRY VERMOUTH
SEA SALT AND FRESHLY GROUND
    BLACK PEPPER
SMALL BUNCH OF FRESH
    PARSLEY, TO FINISH

1   Bring the water to the boil in a kettle.

2   Melt the butter in a large saucepan and snip the spring onions into the butter. Add the cumin.

3   Rinse the carrots and finely shred them in the food processor, using the shredding blade. Add to the pan and soften for a couple of minutes over a moderate heat.

4   Zest, then juice the orange. Stir the zest and vermouth into the carrot mixture.

5   Pour in the boiling water and simmer for 5 minutes.

6   Add the orange juice and season to taste. Snip a little parsley over the soup to finish.

Clockwise from the top left: Carrot and Orange Soup; Lettuce and Pea Soup (page 37); Chinese soup (page 41)

CAULIFLOWER SOUP

This is a very filling soup which can be a meal in itself, served with Croutons (see page 61) or buttered toast rubbed with garlic. Best results are obtained using a firm fresh cauliflower and a strong-flavoured mature farmhouse Cheddar.

1 LARGE CAULIFLOWER
75G/2½OZ BUTTER
575ML/1PT CHICKEN STOCK
300ML/½PT MILK
PINCH OF DRIED MARJORAM
115G/4OZ MATURE CHEDDAR
NUTMEG
SEA SALT AND FRESHLY GROUND
  BLACK PEPPER

1 Roughly chop the cauliflower into florets and whizz to crumbs in the food processor.

2 Melt 50g/2oz of the butter in a large saucepan and sauté the processed cauliflower over a moderate heat.

3 Add the chicken stock, milk and dried marjoram. Bring to the boil, then reduce the heat and simmer for a few minutes, stirring frequently.

4 Grate in the cheese along with nutmeg to taste and stir them in well.

5 Season to taste and finish by adding the remaining butter, cut into small pieces.

GARLIC SOUP

We have broken our 10-minute rule to include this recipe – even if the soup needs to simmer for 15 minutes – as it requires virtually no preparation. It is adapted from *The Cuisine of Paul Bocuse* and when we first read and tried it, we could not believe that anything quite so basic could taste so complex – but it does!

1.75L/3PT WATER
15 GARLIC CLOVES
2 CLOVES
3 FRESH SAGE LEAVES
2 TSP SEA SALT
1 FRENCH STICK
115G/4OZ GRUYÈRE OR
  PARMESAN
OLIVE OIL
FRESHLY GROUND BLACK
  PEPPER

1 Heat the oven to 250C/475F/gas9.

2 Bring the water to the boil with the garlic, cloves, sage, salt and pepper. Leave to simmer for 15 minutes.

3 Meanwhile, slice the French bread and place it on a baking sheet.

4 Grate the cheese and scatter it over the bread along with a few drops of olive oil.

5 Bake in the oven until golden brown.

6 Place a couple of slices of the cooked bread in each soup plate, if necessary adjust the seasoning of the hot soup and pour it into the plates.

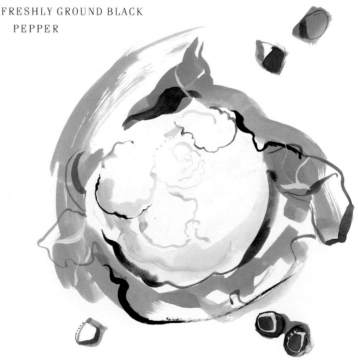

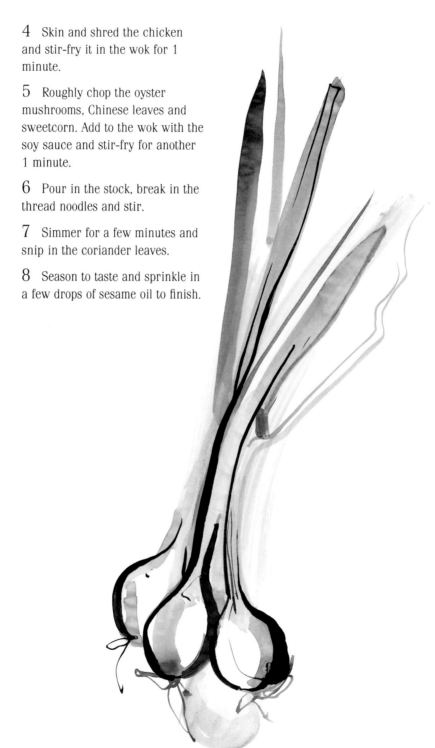

CHINESE SOUP

For super-fast stir-frying remember to shred or chop the ingredients very finely (see page 30). One short cut you cannot take is to use a stock cube in this soup. A good stock, either home-made or a bought Fonds de Cuisine (see page 34), is vital.

1.1L/2PT CHICKEN STOCK
2 GARLIC CLOVES
3 SPRING ONIONS
PIECE OF FRESH GINGER, ABOUT 2.5CM/1IN
2 TBSP SUNFLOWER OIL
1 LARGE BONED CHICKEN BREAST
115G/4OZ OYSTER MUSHROOMS
1 HEAD OF CHINESE LEAVES (OR 1 COS LETTUCE)
115G/4OZ BABY SWEETCORN
1 TBSP SOY SAUCE
115G/4OZ THREAD NOODLES
SMALL BUNCH OF CORIANDER LEAVES
SEA SALT AND FRESHLY GROUND BLACK PEPPER
FEW DROPS OF SESAME OIL, TO FINISH

1 Bring the stock to the boil, reduce the heat and simmer gently.

2 In the food processor, whizz the garlic, spring onions and ginger to a paste.

3 Heat the oil in a wok until very hot, add the paste and stir-fry for 1 minute.

4 Skin and shred the chicken and stir-fry it in the wok for 1 minute.

5 Roughly chop the oyster mushrooms, Chinese leaves and sweetcorn. Add to the wok with the soy sauce and stir-fry for another 1 minute.

6 Pour in the stock, break in the thread noodles and stir.

7 Simmer for a few minutes and snip in the coriander leaves.

8 Season to taste and sprinkle in a few drops of sesame oil to finish.

Pasta

We would be quite lost without pasta – it is one of our staples. We eat it several times a week, and often serve it when we are entertaining friends.

The time-consuming part of pasta cooking is heating the large quantity of water required (you need about 1.1 litres/2 pints water for each 115g/4oz serving of pasta), but this can be greatly reduced if you boil the water in 2 halves: one in the pasta pan and the other in a large kettle.

Fresh pasta is currently enjoying great popularity and does cook very fast, but – unless it is made in front of our eyes – we are not convinced that it warrants the extra cost. We like the bite and taste of a good dried pasta, and we usually buy packets of one or other of the better known Italian brands made from hard durum wheat.

Depending on the shape you choose, the pasta may take a good 10 minutes to cook. We serve ours in the Italian manner 'al dente' – just tender, but still with a bit of bite – which suits our very fast sauces.

Appetites and tastes vary, so we do not give exact quantities of pasta. However, a good guide is about 85-115g/3-4oz per portion.

Tagliatelle with Sun-dried Tomato and Black Olive Sauce (page 44)

Our Store-cupboard and No-cook Sauces are robust and extremely simple to prepare. We have also included a few extra sauces in 12 Things to do with Tins (see page 20) or you may like to try dressing pasta with some of the sauces or savoury butters from the Fish and Meat chapters (see pages 86 and 101).

STORE-CUPBOARD SAUCES

Simply use the store-cupboard preparations from page 18 as a sauce. You may, perhaps, add an extra ingredient (such as sliced mushrooms) or a herb or two (such as a couple of snipped leaves of fresh – or a small pinch of dried – basil, tarragon or oregano). These sauces need no cooking: just return the cooked and drained pasta to the pan over a very low heat, pour in the store-cupboard sauce of your choice and stir well into the pasta. The heat from the pasta warms the sauce through.

1 LABNA CHEESE BALLS IN OIL

Pour some of the oil from the jar over the pasta. Mix it in well, season to taste with freshly ground black pepper and then add a few whole or crushed labna balls.

2 SUN-DRIED TOMATO AND BLACK OLIVES

Snip 5 or 6 sun-dried tomatoes and a few stoned black olives. Pour some of the oil from the jar over the pasta, add the tomatoes and olives and mix well. Season to taste with sea salt and freshly ground black pepper.

3 CHILLI OIL AND FRESH CORIANDER

Snip some fresh coriander. Pour some chilli oil (or a mixture of chilli and olive oil) over the pasta, add the coriander and mix well. Season with sea salt.

4 ROASTED GARLIC AND PARSLEY

Snip some fresh parsley. Crush some cloves from a head of roasted garlic to extract the purée and add this to the parsley. Pour some good olive oil over the pasta, add the garlic and parsley and mix well. Season with freshly ground black pepper.

NO-COOK SAUCES

Nothing could be easier to make – or fresher tasting – than a no-cook sauce. You mix it into the cooked and drained pasta in exactly the same way as you would a store-cupboard sauce. The residual heat is enough to warm it through and lightly cook it, should that be necessary.

1 CRÈME FRAÎCHE WITH DILL AND SALMON EGGS

Snip a handful of fresh dill over a large (300ml/½pt) carton of crème fraîche. Season with freshly ground black pepper and stir well. Mix into the cooked and drained pasta. Top each serving with a spoonful of salmon eggs.

2 BLUE CHEESE, CREAM AND ROCKET

In the food processor, whizz 85g/3oz blue cheese, a handful of rocket leaves (reserving a few whole ones) and a small (150ml/¼pt) carton of single cream to a thickish sauce. Mix into the cooked and drained pasta, snip over the remaining rocket leaves. Season with freshly ground black pepper.

3 FRESH TOMATO AND MINT

In the food processor, roughly whizz about 450g/1lb ripe fresh tomatoes, 1 spring onion, 1 garlic clove and a handful of mint leaves. Stir in a little olive oil. Season with sea salt, freshly ground black pepper and a pinch of sugar, if the tomatoes aren't sweet enough. Mix into the cooked and drained pasta.

4 RAW EGG, PARMA HAM AND CHIVES

Beat a couple of eggs with a crushed garlic clove and a small (150ml/¼pt) carton of single cream. Snip some Parma ham and chives into the mixture. Stir into the cooked and drained pasta. Season with freshly ground black pepper.

5 ANCHOVY, CAPERS, PARSLEY AND THYME

Snip 3 or 4 anchovy fillets with 1 tablespoon each of fresh parsley and thyme. Add some drained capers and olive oil. Stir into the cooked and drained pasta. Season with freshly ground black pepper.

6 WALNUT AND THYME

In the food processor, whizz a handful of walnuts to a smooth paste. Add a few sprigs of fresh thyme, a couple of eggs, some lemon zest, sea salt and freshly ground black pepper to taste and whizz again to blend. Add 1 or 2 tablespoons of olive oil and stir into the cooked and drained pasta.

7 SPINACH, CREAM CHEESE AND PARMESAN

In the food processor, whizz 140g/
5oz cream cheese and 50g/2oz
Parmesan until smooth. Add about
225g/½lb baby spinach leaves and
a small carton (150ml/¼pt) of fresh
single cream and whizz again
briefly. Stir into the cooked and
drained pasta.

8 SHREDDED COURGETTES WITH PINE KERNELS AND TARRAGON

Shred 1 or 2 courgettes in the food processor, using the shredding blade. Snip over a few tarragon leaves and add a handful of pine kernels and 1 or 2 tablespoons of olive oil. Season with sea salt and freshly ground black pepper. Mix into the cooked and drained pasta.

Left: Shredded Courgettes with Pine Kernels and Tarragon over fusilli; Right: Crème Fraîche with Dill and Salmon Eggs (page 45) over plain tagliatelle.

Eggs

Egg dishes are a useful stand-by in 10-minute cuisine as practically everyone has half a dozen eggs in the refrigerator.

We have already mentioned in the introductory section on ingredients that we only buy eggs from trusted suppliers who can guarantee them to be totally safe. It is also a good idea to check each egg by first breaking it into a separate container.

All the following recipes are for four 'size 2' or 'size 3' eggs. Allow 1 per person for a half-plate portion and 2 for a full plate.

Parsley, Chive and Tarragon Eggs
(page 50)

STIR-FRIED EGGS

These are a sort of cross between scrambled eggs and an omelette, although stir-fried eggs are cooked at a higher temperature in a wok. It helps the process if the eggs are at room temperature before being cooked, and the oil (ideally sunflower, grapeseed or light olive) should be well heated before adding the eggs.

First beat the eggs with a little extra liquid (water or chicken or vegetable stock) then pour this mixture into the heated oil in the wok. Using a scoop or chopsticks, keep the eggs on the move. The result is delicately flavoured golden strips of lightly cooked eggs.

BASIC STIR-FRIED EGGS

Heat 1 tablespoon of oil in a wok until hot, swirling it around. Lightly beat 4 eggs with 2 tablespoons water or chicken or vegetable stock. Season to taste with sea salt and freshly ground black pepper. Pour into the wok and stir-fry until the eggs are just cooked and golden in colour.

1 MUSHROOM, SPRING ONION AND CORIANDER EGGS

Heat 1 tablespoon of oil in a wok and swirl it around. Add a pinch of crushed coriander seeds and a handful of finely chopped mushrooms. Snip in 1-2 spring onions and stir-fry for a minute or two. Lightly beat 4 eggs with 2 tablespoons of water or stock, season and pour into the wok. Stir-fry until the eggs are cooked.

2 PARSLEY, CHIVE AND TARRAGON EGGS

Heat 2 tablespoons of oil with a knob of butter in a wok and swirl it around. Lightly beat 4 eggs with 2 tablespoons of water or stock, season, snip in a handful of the herbs and pour into the wok. Stir-fry until the eggs are cooked.

3 PRAWNS, GINGER AND SHERRY EGGS

Heat 1 tablespoon of oil in a wok and swirl it around. Add a crushed garlic clove and a finely chopped piece of ginger (about 2.5cm/1in) and stir-fry for a minute or two. Tip in a handful of peeled cooked prawns and stir-fry for 1 minute. Lightly beat 4 eggs with 1 tablespoon each of water and sherry, add a dash of soy sauce, season and pour into the wok. Stir-fry until the eggs are cooked.

4 OLIVE, SUN-DRIED TOMATO AND HERB EGGS

Heat 1 tablespoon of olive oil in a wok and swirl it around. Lightly beat 4 eggs with 2 tablespoons of water or stock and season. Add a few stoned and chopped black olives, snip in a couple of sun-dried tomatoes and a few sprigs each of fresh marjoram and oregano. Pour into the wok and stir-fry until the eggs are cooked.

5 SMOKED TROUT AND DILL EGGS

Heat 2 tablespoons of oil with a knob of butter in a wok and swirl it around. Lightly beat 4 eggs with 2 tablespoons of water or stock. Season, add a few slivers of smoked trout and snip in some dill. Pour into the wok and stir-fry until the eggs are cooked. Then beat in 1 or 2 tablespoons of sour cream.

6 HAM AND LEEK EGGS

Heat 1 tablespoon of oil in a wok and swirl it around. Add the finely chopped white of 1 leek and stir-fry for 1 minute. Lightly beat 4 eggs with 2 tablespoons water or stock and 1 teaspoon of mustard and season. Snip in a slice of ham, pour into the wok and stir-fry until the eggs are cooked.

EGGAHS

They are a sort of cross between a quiche filling and an omelette. Our eggahs are cooked in a heavy-based omelette pan and then finished off under the grill.

In order for them to be crisp on the outside while still moist and barely set inside, eggahs must be about 5cm/2in thick. For our 4-egg eggah we use a 17cm/7in pan.

Either stir the filling into the mixture and cook it like a thick omelette or sauté the filling separately in the pan, pour the eggs on top and then lift the filling to allow the eggs to set underneath.

BASIC EGGAH

In a heavy-based omelette pan, heat 1 tablespoon of oil with a knob of butter. Stir in any cooked and chopped suitable leftovers (chicken, potatoes, peas, salmon, etc) and sauté for 1 minute. Beat 4 eggs with a tablespoon of milk, season with sea salt and freshly ground black pepper and pour over the filling, lifting it to allow the mixture to run underneath. Cook until just set, then sprinkle with a little extra oil or dot with butter and brown under a hot grill.

1 TWO-CHEESE EGGAH

In a heavy-based omelette pan, heat 2 teaspoons of oil with a knob of butter. Beat 4 eggs with 1 tablespoon of milk. Stir in a handful each of Mozzarella and Parmesan cheeses, cut into slivers, and season. Pour into the pan and cook until set. Sprinkle with extra cheese and brown under the grill.

2 BLUE CHEESE AND SPRING ONION EGGAH

In a heavy-based omelette pan, heat 2 teaspoons of oil with a knob of butter. Beat 4 eggs with 1 tablespoon of milk. Crumble in 50g/2oz blue cheese. Snip in 1 spring onion and season. Pour into the pan and cook until set. Sprinkle with extra cheese and brown under the grill.

3 COURGETTE, TOMATO AND THYME EGGAH

In a heavy-based omelette pan, heat 1 tablespoon of olive oil with a knob of butter. Stir in 2 tablespoons each of chopped courgettes and tomatoes, snip in a few sprigs of fresh thyme and cook for a couple of minutes to soften. Beat 4 eggs with 1 tablespoon of milk. Season, pour into the pan and cook until set. Sprinkle with olive oil and brown under the grill.

4 OYSTER MUSHROOM EGGAH

In a heavy-based omelette pan, heat 1 tablespoon of olive oil with a knob of butter. Stir in a handful of sliced oyster mushrooms with a crushed ½ garlic clove and sauté for 1 or 2 minutes. Beat 4 eggs with 1 tablespoon of milk. Season, pour into the pan and cook until set. Dot with butter and brown under the grill.

5 ASPARAGUS TIP AND CREAM CHEESE EGGAH

In a heavy-based omelette pan, heat 2 teaspoons of oil with a knob of butter. Stir in a handful of asparagus tips and sauté for a couple of minutes. Beat 4 eggs with 1 tablespoon each of milk and cream cheese. Season, pour into the pan and cook until set. Dot with cream cheese and brown.

6 SPINACH AND PARMESAN EGGAH

In a heavy-based omelette pan, heat 2 teaspoons of oil with a knob of butter. Snip in a handful of washed and well-drained spinach and sweat for 1 minute. Beat 4 eggs with 1 tablespoon each of milk and single cream. Grate in a small piece of Parmesan and a little nutmeg. Season, pour into the pan and cook until set. Sprinkle with more Parmesan and brown.

EGGS EN COCOTTE

For this classic dish, in which eggs are baked in buttered ramekins set in a bain marie in the oven, use a baking tray half-filled with water which has been boiled in a kettle to speed up the process.

One egg en cocotte is a half-plate portion, and 2 a full plate. As well as the recipes below, try eggs en cocotte with Hollandaise Sauce (see page 84) or our flavoured butters (see pages 86-7 and 101).

BASIC EGGS EN COCOTTE

Heat the oven to 180C/350F/gas4 and boil a kettle. Divide 45g/1½oz butter into 4 pieces and spread each into one of 4 small ramekins, ensuring that the sides and bases are all well greased.

Snip a few chopped chives into each ramekin and then trickle 2 teaspoons of single cream into each. Break an egg into each ramekin and trickle a little more cream over that. Season lightly and put the ramekins in a baking tray.

Pour boiling water from the kettle into the baking tray to come halfway up the sides of the ramekins. Bake for 7-10 minutes — the exact timing depends on how you like your eggs to be cooked.

Watercress, Herb and Cream Cheese Eggs

1 MUSHROOM, SHALLOT AND CREAM EGGS

Finely chop about 50g/2oz mushrooms and 1 shallot. Put equal portions of this mixture into each ramekin. Trickle over a little single cream and season. Break an egg into each ramekin and then trickle over a little extra cream. Bake as above.

2 CREAM AND CHEESE EGGS

Into each ramekin, put about 1 tablespoon of grated Gruyère. Trickle over a little double cream, add a drop or two of Kirsch and season. Break 1 egg into each ramekin and trickle over a little extra cream and a sprinkling of grated cheese. Bake as above.

3 CURD CHEESE, CHILLI AND CUMIN EGGS

Beat 115g/4oz curd cheese with a small pinch each of ground cumin, turmeric and chilli powder. Into each ramekin spread some of the mixture. Break 1 egg into each ramekin and dot with a little butter. Bake as above.

4 SMOKED HADDOCK AND CREAM EGGS

Into each ramekin, place some small pieces of smoked haddock. Trickle over a little single cream and season with cayenne pepper. Break 1 egg into each ramekin and trickle over a little extra cream. Bake as above.

5 SPINACH AND ANCHOVY EGGS

Into each ramekin, put some finely chopped spinach, capers and anchovy fillet. Trickle over a little single cream and season with freshly ground black pepper. Break 1 egg into each ramekin and dot with a little butter. Bake as above.

6 WATERCRESS, HERB AND CREAM CHEESE EGGS

Into each ramekin, put some finely chopped watercress, parsley, savory and lemon balm. Spoon in a little cream cheese and season. Break 1 egg into each ramekin and dot with extra cream cheese. Bake as above.

Salads

For us, there is no such thing as a meal without a salad: as a starter, a main course or a side dish. We eat at least one salad every day, and soon suffer serious withdrawal symptoms if we have to go without.

Luckily, the range of salad leaves generally available in this country has improved enormously in the last few years and now most major supermarket chains stock a reasonably good selection.

The following leaves and herbs are all widely available and a good bet in season: cos, webb, little gem, butterhead, iceberg, lollo rosso and oakleaf lettuces; chicories including curly endive (or frisée), Belgian endive (or Brussels chicory), Batavian endive (or escarole), treviso and radicchio; lamb's lettuce (also known as corn salad or mâche), rocket, watercress, baby spinach, sorrel, dandelion leaves and purslane.

Most supermarkets also now sell growing herbs in plastic containers, which can be kept on the window sill. Fresh parsley, chives and coriander we sometimes snip into dressings; chives, thyme, basil, chervil, coriander, sage, tarragon, summer and winter savory, borage, hyssop, parsley, mint, marjoram and oregano we snip over the leaves.

Flowers or seed tops, such as hyssop, nasturtium, chives, rocket, radish pods and spinach heads, can also be used whole or snipped into salads.

Whatever the mix, remember to wash and spin-dry everything thoroughly (see page 25), as soggy leaves water down the dressing. Tearing and trimming leaves with the hands is better and easier.

Sealed plastic sachets of ready trimmed and washed mixed salad leaves are also now readily available. These are expensive, with a short shelf life (do check for any discoloration before buying!), but they can save precious time.

When making up a salad, bear in mind the colour, taste and texture balance and use a good variety of different types of leaves for an interesting combination.

For extra crunch, sprinkle the leaves with sea salt.

You may have noticed that some old stand-bys, such as tomatoes, cucumber, carrots, white and red cabbage, red and green peppers, radishes and beetroot are missing from our list. We have not included them because we don't feel that they belong in a mixed-leaf salad.

DOLLOP DRESSINGS

These are a cross between a salad dressing and a dip, and are best spooned on the side of the plate rather than tossed into a salad. Alternatively, heap the dollop of dressing on a pile of leaves – but make no attempt at coating! We particularly like these dressings with grated vegetables and crudité sticks and florets.

1 MAYONNAISE

In a food processor, whizz 2 egg yolks with 1 tablespoon of lemon juice and 1 teaspoon of mustard. With the food processor running, trickle in 300ml/½pt mixed olive and sunflower oil and process until thick and creamy. Add 1 teaspoon of lemon juice or water, whizz again and season with sea salt and freshly ground black pepper.

2 CREAM MAYONNAISE

As Mayonnaise above, but at the end add 2 tablespoons of single cream instead of the extra 1 teaspoon of lemon juice or water.

3 HERB MAYONNAISE

As Mayonnaise above, but add a handful of herbs, such as parsley, chives, tarragon and marjoram, with the lemon juice or water.

4 BLUE CHEESE DRESSING

Whizz a generous piece (about 85g/3oz) of blue cheese with 3 tablespoons of sour cream, 2 tablespoons of olive oil, 1 teaspoon of lemon juice and freshly ground black pepper until smooth.

COATING DRESSINGS

The most important thing for any dressing, especially one which is to coat all the leaves, is the quality of the ingredients – only the best oils, such as extra-virgin olive oil, will do. This is not as extravagant as it sounds since you do not need much.

One essential point is always to use a big enough salad bowl to be able to toss the salad comfortably. First mix your dressing in a small bowl or jug until well blended and then either pour it into the empty salad bowl, adding the leaves on top, or pour it over the salad in the bowl. Either way, toss it in the bowl until all the leaves are well coated.

(We tend to use our hands to dress the salads, which is very easy and efficient.) We also like our salads just lightly coated, so we have no hard and fast rules about quantities. In this chapter, however – as elsewhere in the book – all our recipes are for 4 people.

How much dressing is needed depends entirely on how lightly or generously coated you like your salad to be. A good guideline, however, is 6 tablespoons of dressing for each 350g/12oz salad leaves. Go easy on the vinegar: no more than 2 tablespoons of those 6 should be vinegar! Our favourite ratio is 5:1 oil to vinegar. Sea salt we use more liberally in salad dressings than in any other type of dish: one trick is to go on adding salt to the dressing, in small amounts, until it stops tasting oily.

1 POUR-OVER DRESSING

Trickle a good oil (see above) over a salad and toss. Add a pinch of sea salt, freshly ground black pepper and, if you like, a squirt of fresh lemon juice. Toss again.

2 VINAIGRETTE

In a cup, mix together 5 tablespoons of olive oil with 1 tablespoon of white wine vinegar, 1 teaspoon of mustard and sea salt and freshly ground black pepper to taste.

3 GARLIC VINAIGRETTE

As for Vinaigrette, but add 1 small crushed garlic clove.

4 HERB VINAIGRETTE

As for Vinaigrette, but add a handful of snipped chives or tarragon leaves.

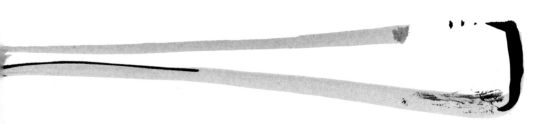

5 EGG VINAIGRETTE

In a cup, beat together 1 egg yolk with 1 teaspoon of mustard and 1 teaspoon of lemon juice. Slowly trickle in 6 tablespoons of olive oil, beating continuously. Season.

6 CREAM VINAIGRETTE

In a cup, combine 1 tablespoon of single cream with 2 teaspoons of sherry vinegar. Beat in 5 tablespoons of olive oil and season.

7 ANCHOVY VINAIGRETTE

Snip a couple of drained anchovy fillets into a small bowl and add 1 small crushed garlic clove. Beat in 5 tablespoons of olive oil, 2 teaspoons of lemon juice and season.

8 TAHINI DRESSING

In a cup, beat 2 tablespoons of tahini with 5 tablespoons of yoghurt, the juice of $\frac{1}{2}$ a lemon, $\frac{1}{2}$ a crushed garlic clove, a pinch of ground cumin and sea salt and freshly ground black pepper.

Herb Hamburger (page 100); served with Mushroom Butter (page 101) and a green salad dressed with Egg Vinaigrette, Croutons and Flaked Almonds (page 61)

9 ORIENTAL DRESSING

In a cup, beat 3 tablespoons of soy sauce with 3 tablespoons of water, 2 teaspoons of sesame oil and 1 teaspoon of ground ginger.

10 SOY SAUCE DRESSING

Snip a handful of fresh coriander leaves into a cup. Mix in 2 tablespoons of soy sauce, 2 tablespoons of water, 1 tablespoon of sunflower oil, 1 teaspoon of sherry vinegar, 2 teaspoons of mustard and a pinch of sugar.

11 TOMATO AND CHILLI DRESSING

In the food processor, whizz a ripe tomato with 1 tablespoon of wine vinegar, 2 tablespoons of chilli oil, a pinch of sugar, and season to taste with sea salt and freshly ground black pepper.

12 CORIANDER AND PARSLEY DRESSING

Snip $\frac{1}{2}$ a spring onion and a handful each of coriander and parsley leaves into a bowl. Mix in the juice of $\frac{1}{2}$ a lemon, 3 tablespoons of olive oil and 3 tablespoons of single cream and season to taste with sea salt and freshly ground black pepper.

BITS & PIECES FOR SALADS

Scatter these on top of a mixed, dressed and tossed salad to add extra crunch and flavour and to improve appearance.

For interesting salads, experiment with combinations of more than one item at a time, such as Croutons, Parmesan and Black Olives.

Remember, however, that some of these toppings may be very salty, so cut down on the sea salt accordingly when seasoning the salad.

1 AVOCADO

Peel, stone and chop a ripe avocado and sprinkle the flesh liberally with lemon juice. Good with spinach, chicory and other bitter leaves, and works well with Croutons and Anchovy Vinaigrette.

2 MANGE-TOUT PEAS

Blanch a handful of trimmed mange-tout peas for 1 or 2 minutes. Drain, refresh in cold water and dry. These add an interesting contrast of texture to most salads and are especially good with Baby Sweetcorn and Tahini Dressing.

3 BROCCOLI

Trim a head or two of broccoli into tiny florets. Blanch for 1 or 2 minutes. Drain, refresh in cold water and dry. Good with Black Olives and Tomato and Chilli Dressing, or a strongly flavoured oil such as walnut or sesame.

4 BABY SWEETCORN

Chop a handful of baby sweetcorn. Blanch for 1 or 2 minutes. Drain, refresh in cold water and dry. These add texture and a touch of sweetness and are especially good with Oriental Dressing.

5 STRAWBERRIES

Halve or quarter some ripe strawberries and sprinkle with black pepper. These look particularly pretty on top of an early summer leaf salad and are especially refreshing with chopped mint and Vinaigrette.

6 ORANGE

Peel and thinly slice a couple of oranges. Good with chicory, tarragon and Walnuts and Cream Vinaigrette.

7 BLACK OLIVES

Stone and chop a handful of black olives and toss into a dressed salad. Good with fennel or lettuce and Garlic Vinaigrette.

8 PARMESAN

Sprinkle some grated Parmesan over a dressed leaf salad. Good with mixed lettuces and Anchovy Vinaigrette.

9 LABNA BALLS

Crumble a few labna balls over the salad, using the oil from the jar as a dressing (see page 18). Good with chicory, rocket and other winter leaves.

10 BLUE CHEESE

Break a piece of blue cheese into small pieces and sprinkle over a dressed leaf salad. Especially good with spinach or dandelion leaves and Vinaigrette.

11 WALNUTS

Chop a handful of walnuts. These add an interesting richness to winter leaves and watercress and are especially good with Cream Vinaigrette.

12 FLAKED ALMONDS

Heat a little oil in a frying pan. Add a handful of flaked almonds and sauté them until golden brown. Drain on kitchen paper and sprinkle with sea salt. Good with sweet summer leaves and Egg Vinaigrette.

13 PINE KERNELS

Heat a little oil in a frying pan. Add a handful of pine kernels and sauté them for 1 or 2 minutes. Drain on kitchen paper. Good with a herby salad and Garlic Vinaigrette.

14 HAZELNUTS

Grill a handful of hazelnuts for a few minutes, shaking the grill pan a couple of times so they brown evenly. Sprinkle with sea salt. Good with lettuces and curly endive, this is among the best and simplest salad dressings.

15 PISTACHIOS

Grill a handful of shelled pistachios for a couple of minutes to heat them through. Sprinkle with sea salt. Good with Cream Vinaigrette.

16 POPPY SEEDS

Sprinkle a generous handful of poppy seeds over a dressed salad. Good with spring onions and Egg Vinaigrette.

17 SESAME SEEDS

Toast a handful of sesame seeds in a dry frying pan for 1 or 2 minutes and sprinkle over a dressed salad. Good with Oriental Dressing.

18 SUNFLOWER SEEDS

Toast a handful of sunflower seeds in a dry frying pan for 2 or 3 minutes. Sprinkle with sea salt and toss into a dressed salad. Good with a mild sweetish salad and Cream Vinaigrette.

19 DILL AND FENNEL SEEDS

Mix a pinch each of dill and fennel seeds with some sea salt and a drop or 2 of lemon juice. Toss into a dressed salad. Good with bitter leaves and Vinaigrette.

20 CROUTONS

Cut off the crusts from a couple of slices of bread, then cut the bread into small squares. Rub the inside of a frying pan with a clove of garlic, heat a little olive oil and a knob of butter in it and fry the bread until evenly crisp and golden. Drain on kitchen paper. A good all-rounder, adding great texture and pungency.

STARTER & MAIN COURSE SALADS

Normally most of our dishes work just as well as main courses as they do as starters. However, in the case of salads, some – such as Melon, Carrot and Lime Juice, Courgette Basil, and Leek – are meant only as starters and will not do as main courses.

MELON SALAD

Use whichever variety of melon is in season, the riper the better.

½ SMALL ONION
1 TBSP SUGAR
1 TSP MUSTARD POWDER
2 TBSP WHITE WINE VINEGAR
75ML/4 TBSP SUNFLOWER OIL
1 MELON
1 ORANGE
1 LARGE PEAR
225G/8OZ CURLY ENDIVE
  LEAVES
1 TBSP POPPY SEEDS

1 Whizz the onion, sugar, mustard powder, white wine vinegar and oil until smooth.

2 Pour the dressing into a bowl and chill in the freezer while preparing the salad.

3 Quarter the melon and remove the seeds. Run a knife between the skin and flesh to separate the flesh and then cut it into slices.

4 Peel the orange and separate into segments.

5 Peel and quarter the pear. Remove the core and cut the flesh into slices.

6 Arrange the curly endive leaves in a large salad bowl.

7 Scatter the prepared fruits over the top.

8 Sprinkle the chilled dressing over the salad followed by the poppy seeds.

CHICKEN LIVER AND CHILLI SALAD

●

225G/8OZ CHICKEN LIVERS
3 TBSP CHILLI OIL AND ½ CHILLI
  IN OIL (SEE PAGE 19)
1 GARLIC CLOVE
1 SPRING ONION
SMALL HANDFUL OF CORIANDER
  LEAVES
350G/12OZ MIXED SALAD
  LEAVES
2 TBSP OLIVE OIL
25G/1OZ BUTTER
2 TBSP WHITE WINE VINEGAR
SEA SALT AND FRESHLY GROUND
  BLACK PEPPER

1 Trim and slice the chicken livers. Rinse and pat them dry with kitchen paper.

2 In a sauté pan, heat the chilli oil.

3 Finely chop the garlic clove and the chilli from the oil. Add these to the pan.

4 Snip in the spring onion and the coriander. Add the chicken livers, stir and sauté the mixture over a moderate heat for a few minutes, depending on how pink the livers are to be.

5 Meanwhile, wash and spin-dry the salad leaves. Tip them into a salad bowl and sprinkle them with olive oil and sea salt.

6 Using a slotted spoon, remove the chicken livers from the pan and add them to the leaves.

7 Add the butter to the pan and swirl until melted. Pour in the vinegar and turn up the heat. Using a wooden spoon, scrape the sediment in the pan to deglaze it until most of the vinegar has been boiled off.

8 Pour the deglazed pan juices over the salad and season.

Chicken Liver and Chilli Salad

CARROT AND LIME JUICE SALAD

◑

To save time use small sweet young carrots, as they do not require peeling.

350G/12OZ YOUNG CARROTS
3 SPRING ONIONS
PIECE OF FRESH GINGER,
   ABOUT 2.5CM/1IN ACROSS
6 TBSP CHILLI OIL
JUICE OF ½ LIME
SEA SALT

1 Rinse the carrots and grate in the food processor, using the shredding blade. Tip into a salad bowl.

2 Snip the spring onions over a small bowl. Grate in the ginger, add the oil and lime juice. Season with salt and whisk together.

3 Pour the dressing over the salad and toss.

COURGETTE AND BASIL SALAD

◑

Again, use young vegetables – not only do large courgettes need peeling, but they are inclined to have a poor watery texture and a slightly bitter taste.

350G/12OZ BABY COURGETTES
1 GARLIC CLOVE
8 TBSP OLIVE OIL
1 LEMON
HANDFUL OF BASIL LEAVES
SEA SALT AND FRESHLY GROUND
   BLACK PEPPER

1 Rinse the courgettes and grate with the garlic in the food processor, using the shredding blade.

2 Warm 6 tablespoons of the oil in a sauté pan and tip in the courgettes.

3 Squeeze the juice from the lemon and add this juice to the pan. Stir for a couple of minutes and season with salt and pepper.

4 Tip into a salad bowl and sprinkle in a little extra oil. Snip over the basil leaves and toss.

LEEK SALAD

◑

450G/1LB LEEKS
2 EGGS
2 SPRING ONIONS
SMALL BUNCH OF FLAT-LEAF
   PARSLEY
1 TBSP CAPERS
6 TBSP OLIVE OIL
2 TBSP RED WINE VINEGAR
SEA SALT AND FRESHLY GROUND
   BLACK PEPPER

1 Boil a kettle.

2 Meanwhile, rinse and trim the leeks and then slice them.

3 Pour some of the boiling water into a saucepan, add the eggs and boil for 6 minutes.

4 Pour the rest of the boiling water into another saucepan, add leeks and simmer for 1-2 minutes.

5 Drain the leeks and pat dry.

6 Snip the spring onions and parsley into a small bowl and add the capers.

7 Shell the eggs under cold running water, snip them into the bowl and mix together with a fork.

8 Add the oil and vinegar to the bowl, season and beat the dressing together well.

9 Arrange the leeks on a plate and pour over the dressing.

Leek Salad

TWO-CHEESE SALAD

●

There is no need to buy expensive farmhouse goats' cheese for this salad, as it is combined with Mozzarella. Choose one of the many factory-made 'logs', carefully remove the rind (which can have an unpleasant taste) and cut the cheese into small slices or slivers.

Make the most of the interesting range of flavoured breads now to be found in many supermarkets, speciality bakers and delicatessens: such as onion, walnut, raisin, olive or garlic.

4 SLICES BREAD, PREFERABLY
  FLAVOURED (SEE ABOVE)
115G/4OZ MOZZARELLA
115G/4OZ GOATS' CHEESE
350G/12OZ MIXED SALAD
  LEAVES
2 TBSP WALNUT OIL
SEA SALT AND FRESHLY GROUND
  BLACK PEPPER

1   Heat the grill and toast the bread on one side.

2   Meanwhile, cut the cheeses into slices, removing any rind.

3   Put a slice of Mozzarella on the untoasted side of each piece of bread. Cover with a slice of goats' cheese, season with pepper and return to the grill until the cheese has melted and is golden brown.

4   Meanwhile, wash and spin-dry the salad leaves. Tip them out on a plate or into a salad bowl, sprinkle with oil and sea salt and toss.

5   Add the toasted cheese slices to the leaves.

CHICKEN AND SUN-DRIED TOMATO SALAD

●

450ML/¾PT WATER
200ML/7FLOZ DRY WHITE WINE
1 CELERY STICK
1 BAY LEAF
4 BLACK PEPPERCORNS
3 BONED CHICKEN BREASTS
350G/12OZ MIXED SALAD
  LEAVES
4 SUN-DRIED TOMATOES IN OIL
  (SEE PAGE 18)
4 LABNA BALLS IN OIL (SEE
  PAGE 18)
SEA SALT AND FRESHLY GROUND
  BLACK PEPPER

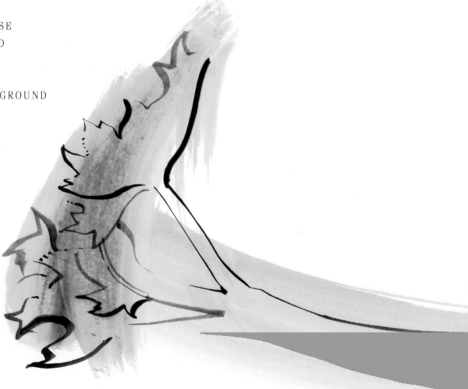

1   In a sauté pan, bring to the boil the water and wine, along with celery, bay leaf and peppercorns. Reduce the heat immediately and leave to simmer.

2   Meanwhile, skin the chicken breasts and cut them in half lengthwise.

3   Add the chicken to the pan and simmer for 6 minutes, or until cooked through.

4   Meanwhile, wash and spin-dry the salad leaves, then tip them into a salad bowl.

5   Snip the sun-dried tomatoes over the leaves and spoon a little of their oil over as well.

6   Crumble the labna balls over the salad and spoon a little of their oil over the salad.

7   Drain the cooked chicken breasts, cut them into strips and add to the salad.

8   Season and toss well together.

EGG AND BLUE CHEESE SALAD

Any leaves work well in this recipe, but it is particularly good with lamb's lettuce and curly endive.

If you cannot find Roquefort, buy any strong-flavoured creamy blue cheese.

350G/12OZ MIXED SALAD
   LEAVES
25G/1OZ BUTTER
4 RASHERS SMOKED STREAKY
   BACON
75G/3OZ ROQUEFORT OR OTHER
   BLUE CHEESE
FEW SPRIGS OF FRESH THYME
4 TBSP WHITE WINE
4 TBSP SINGLE CREAM
DASH OF VINEGAR
4 EGGS
FRESHLY GROUND BLACK
   PEPPER

1   Bring a large saucepan of water to the boil.

2   Wash and spin-dry the salad leaves and tip them into a salad bowl.

3   Melt the butter in a sauté pan. Snip in the bacon and sauté for a couple of minutes over a moderate heat.

4   Crumble in the cheese and stir until it starts to melt.

5   Snip in the thyme and add the white wine and cream. Stir occasionally until smooth, and then season with pepper.

6   Add the vinegar to the boiling water and reduce the heat to a simmer. Stir the water, crack the eggs into the water one at a time and poach them for 2 or 3 minutes, until the whites are just set.

7   Using a slotted spoon, carefully lift out the poached eggs, drain and put them on top of the salad leaves.

8   Pour over the cheese and bacon dressing.

MUSHROOM SALAD

◑

This salad tastes best if a number of different types of mushroom are used: particularly brown caps and oyster mushrooms and – if the budget runs to it – wild mushrooms, such as chanterelles and ceps.

450G/1LB MIXED MUSHROOMS
   (SEE ABOVE)
1 GARLIC CLOVE
3 TBSP OLIVE OIL
25G/1OZ BUTTER
1 LEMON
SEA SALT AND FRESHLY GROUND
   BLACK PEPPER
SMALL BUNCH OF FRESH
   CHIVES

1   Wipe the mushrooms and slice them if they are large.

2   Rub a sauté pan with the garlic. Heat the oil and sauté the mushrooms over a moderate heat for 2 or 3 minutes, stirring frequently.

3   Cut the butter into small pieces and dot it over the mushrooms. Stir until the butter has melted.

4   Tip the cooked mushrooms out on a suitable dish.

5   Squeeze the juice from the lemon and sprinkle it over the mushrooms.

6   Season with sea salt and pepper. Snip over the chives.

BACON AND BREADCRUMB SALAD

●

Spinach and rocket are our favourite leaves for this salad.

For a nutty taste and texture, make breadcrumbs from day-old wholemeal bread.

4 TBSP OLIVE OIL
4 RASHERS SWEET-CURED
    BACON
350G/12OZ MIXED SALAD
    LEAVES
1 RIPE AVOCADO
JUICE OF ½ LEMON
2 THICK SLICES OF DAY-OLD
    BREAD
SMALL BUNCH OF PARSLEY
FEW SPRIGS OF THYME AND
    MARJORAM
1 GARLIC CLOVE
2 TBSP WHITE WINE VINEGAR
SEA SALT AND FRESHLY GROUND
    BLACK PEPPER

1 Heat half the oil in a medium-sized frying pan. Snip in the bacon and sauté over a moderate heat until cooked.

2 Meanwhile, wash and spin-dry the salad leaves and tip them into a large bowl.

3 Halve, stone, peel and chop the avocado. Add to the bowl and sprinkle with lemon juice and sea salt.

4 Using a slotted spoon, remove the bacon from the pan and add to the salad.

5 In the food processor, whizz the bread with the herbs and garlic to make coarse breadcrumbs.

6 Heat the remaining oil in the pan. Add the prepared breadcrumbs to the pan and stir-fry them until golden.

7 Tip the cooked breadcrumb mixture over the salad.

8 Pour the vinegar into the pan, turn up the heat and scrape the sediment in the pan with a wooden spoon to deglaze until almost all the vinegar has been boiled off.

9 Pour the pan juices over the salad. Season with pepper and toss lightly.

SMOKED SALMON SALAD

◑

Buy smoked salmon off-cuts for this salad. Grill any pieces of skin you may find in the off-cuts and snip them over the dressed salad.

This dressing is very rich, so we prefer to serve this salad as a starter.

1 EGG
285G/10OZ MIXED SALAD
  LEAVES
115G/4OZ SMOKED SALMON
  OFF-CUTS
50G/2OZ COTTAGE CHEESE
2 TSP GREEN PEPPERCORNS
1 LIME
½ LEMON
100ML/4FLOZ SINGLE CREAM
SEA SALT AND FRESHLY GROUND
  BLACK PEPPER
SMALL BUNCH OF FRESH
  CHIVES TO FINISH

1 Hard-boil the egg.

2 Meanwhile, wash and spin-dry the salad leaves. Tip them out on a large plate.

3 Snip the best pieces of salmon off-cuts and set them aside for finishing.

4 In the food processor, whizz the remaining salmon with the cottage cheese and green peppercorns until smooth.

5 Zest and juice the lime and juice the lemon. Mix the lemon and lime juices together and set aside the lime zest.

6 Add the cream and fruit juices to the salmon and whizz again.

7 Peel the hard-boiled egg and chop roughly.

8 Add the chopped egg to the dressing. Season with salt and pepper.

9 Pour the dressing over the salad. Sprinkle with the reserved salmon pieces and lime zest and snip over the chives.

SMOKED TROUT AND DILL SALAD

●

350G/12OZ MIXED SALAD
  LEAVES
4 SMOKED TROUT FILLETS
100ML/4FLOZ CRÈME FRAÎCHE
1 TSP CREAM OF HORSERADISH
1 TSP SWEET MUSTARD
SMALL BUNCH OF FRESH DILL
1 TBSP SUNFLOWER OIL
SEA SALT AND FRESHLY GROUND
  BLACK PEPPER

1 Wash and spin-dry the salad leaves and tip them out on a large plate.

2 Cut the trout fillets into thin strips and put them on top of the leaves.

3 In the food processor, whizz the crème fraîche with the horseradish, mustard, dill and oil until smooth. Season with salt and pepper.

4 Pour the dressing over the salad.

Fish

The most important aspect of cooking fish in 10 minutes starts at the fishmonger's. Make friends with him, and he will trim your preparation time by cleaning, scaling, gutting and filleting the fish when you buy it.

Most supermarkets sell ready-trimmed portion packs of fresh fish. These are relatively expensive, but incredibly convenient.

To cook fresh fish fast, it is essential to use small pieces. Remember, though, that it is all too easy to overcook fish, particularly when poaching: so keep the heat moderate and poach very gently, so that the liquid is just barely bubbling.

Steam-boiled Scallops (page 79)

POACHED SALMON ESCALOPES WITH MANGO

●

This recipe is adapted from one created by Sri Owen, this country's leading Indonesian food writer.

Allow 140-170g/5-6oz salmon per person. Again we suggest using escalopes, as they are boneless and much easier to halve lengthwise.

Use a ripe – but still firm – mango and peel it Indian-style: cut off 2 pieces, one from either side of the stone, then peel off the skin from each piece.

2 TBSP OLIVE OIL
PIECE OF FRESH GINGER,
    ABOUT 2.5CM/1IN ACROSS
2 SHALLOTS
1 GARLIC CLOVE
½ TSP CHILLI POWDER
100ML/4FLOZ WATER
1 TBSP WHITE WINE VINEGAR
1 TBSP ANCHOVY ESSENCE
1 TSP SUGAR
4 SALMON ESCALOPES
SMALL BUNCH OF FRESH
    CORIANDER
1 LARGE MANGO

1   Heat the oil in a wok.

2   Peel the ginger, shallots and garlic.

3   Whizz to a coarse paste in the food processor with the chilli powder.

4   Add the paste to the wok and stir-fry for 1 minute.

5   Pour in the water, vinegar, anchovy essence and sugar and bring to a simmer.

6   Skin the salmon escalopes and divide each into 2 lengthwise. Add to the wok.

7   Snip in the coriander leaves. Cook for 3 minutes, turning the escalopes once. Take off the heat and leave in a warm place to settle for 1-2 minutes.

8   Peel and chop the mango. Arrange the salmon on a warmed plate with the chopped mango and spoon over the cooking juices.

RED MULLET FILLETS WITH OLIVE AND TOMATO

●

Red mullet is fiddly and time-consuming to fillet, so do ask your fishmonger to do it. Allow a good 170g/6oz of fish per person.

As red mullet tend to be on the small side, you may prefer to cook them whole, but allow 1-2 minutes more cooking time on each side.

4 TBSP OLIVE OIL
3 RIPE TOMATOES
2 GARLIC CLOVES
6 STONED BLACK OLIVES
2 SPRING ONIONS
2 TBSP TAPENADE (SEE PAGE
    19)
SMALL BUNCHES OF FRESH
    HERBS TO INCLUDE: THYME,
    MARJORAM AND PARSLEY
4-8 FILLETS OF RED MULLET
    (SEE ABOVE)
SEA SALT AND FRESHLY GROUND
    BLACK PEPPER.

1 Heat the grill until very hot. Heat half the oil in a frying pan.

2 In the food processor, whizz together the tomatoes, garlic, olives and spring onion.

3 Tip the mixture into the pan and stir-fry for 1 minute.

4 Add the tapenade and snip in the herbs.

5 Stir and simmer the mixture for 5 minutes.

6 Meanwhile, paint the mullet fillets with the remaining oil.

7 Grill the fillets for about 3 minutes on each side. The exact timing will depend on preference and the thickness of the fish.

8 Season and serve with the prepared sauce.

PAN-FRIED TUNA WITH ANCHOVY AND CAPERS

●

Fresh tuna is meaty and strong-flavoured and best bought as a steak about 2cm/¾in thick. Allow 140-170g/5-6oz per person. If the steaks come from the middle of the fish, they will be very large and can be cut in 2 as required.

8 ANCHOVY FILLETS
2 GARLIC CLOVES
5 TBSP OLIVE OIL
4 TUNA STEAKS
2 TBSP CAPERS, DRAINED
150ML/5FLOZ WHITE WINE
SMALL BUNCH OF FLAT-LEAF
   PARSLEY
SEA SALT AND FRESHLY GROUND
   BLACK PEPPER

1 Whizz the anchovies and garlic together in the food processor.

2 Heat half the oil in a frying pan.

3 Add the anchovies and garlic and sweat them for 2 minutes.

4 Add the fish and fry for 3-4 minutes on each side. The exact timing will depend on preference and the thickness of the fish.

5 Remove the fish from the pan, put on a warmed plate and keep warm.

6 Add the capers to the pan, pour in the rest of the oil and the wine. Snip in the parsley and season.

7 Stir over a high heat for 1-2 minutes to reduce the sauce a little.

8 Season and pour the sauce over the fish.

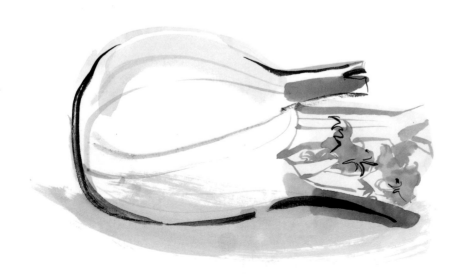

FIVE-SPICE SEARED SALMON

●

If possible, buy salmon escalopes. These are fillets cut lengthwise as opposed to salmon steaks, which are cut across the fish. Look out for escalopes with the skin on, as the skin helps keep the flesh moist and has a good crispy texture when cooked. We generally allow one 140-170g/5-6oz escalope per person and grill it for about 4 minutes on each side.

PIECE OF FRESH GINGER,
    ABOUT 2.5CM/1IN ACROSS
2 SPRING ONIONS
1 LEMON
1 TBSP FIVE-SPICE POWDER
1 TBSP SOY SAUCE
4 SALMON ESCALOPES
SEA SALT

1   Heat the grill until very hot.

2   Meanwhile, peel the ginger, put it in the food processor and roughly snip the spring onions in with it. Whizz to a thick paste.

3   Zest and juice the lemon. Add the lemon juice and zest, five-spice powder and soy sauce to the paste along with salt to taste and whizz briefly.

4   Paste-paint the salmon with the mixture.

5   Grill the salmon, turning the escalopes over once, until evenly cooked. The exact timing will depend on preference and the thickness of the fish.

QUICK-MARINATED SMOKED HADDOCK

For this no-cook recipe, it is essential to use lightly oak-smoked undyed haddock. For the best quality smoked haddock, look out for a fishmonger who sells smoked fillets still joined in pairs; otherwise buy Finnan Haddock and remove its backbone with a sharp knife.

450G/1LB SMOKED HADDOCK
   (SEE ABOVE)
3 SPRING ONIONS
LARGE BUNCH OF FLAT-LEAF
   PARSLEY
1 LEMON
4 TBSP OLIVE OIL
FRESHLY GROUND BLACK
   PEPPER

1 Skin and bone the smoked haddock.

2 Whizz in the food processor until it is in coarse pieces. Tip the prepared fish into a bowl.

3 Snip in the spring onions and parsley.

4 Zest and juice the lemon and add the lemon zest and juice to the bowl with the olive oil. Season with black pepper.

5 Stir the mixture thoroughly and leave to stand for at least 10 minutes.

COD STEAKS WITH MUSTARD

●

Buy cod steaks about 2cm/¾ in thick and allow 170g/5oz per person.

As sometimes happens, the paste may be on the stiff side: spread it with a knife or spatula rather than painting it on.

2 SHALLOTS
1 SLICE OF DAY-OLD BREAD
SMALL BUNCH OF PARSLEY
2 TBSP COARSE-GRAIN MUSTARD
4 TBSP OLIVE OIL
4 COD STEAKS
25G/1OZ BUTTER
75ML/4 TBSP SINGLE CREAM
50ML/3 TBSP WHITE WINE
SEA SALT AND FRESHLY GROUND
   BLACK PEPPER

1 Whizz the shallots, bread and parsley in the food processor.

2 Add half of the mustard and half of the oil. Season and whizz again to a thick coarse paste.

3 Paste-paint the cod with the prepared mixture.

4 Heat the rest of the oil and butter in a frying pan.

5 Add the fish and fry over a moderate heat for 3-4 minutes on each side.

6 Remove the fish from the pan, put on a warmed plate and keep warm.

7 Swirl the cream and wine into the pan along with the rest of the mustard and season to taste.

8 Stir over a high heat for 1 minute to reduce the sauce a little, then pour it over the fish.

STEAM-BOILED SCALLOPS

◑

Allow 1 or 2 medium-sized scallops per person and choose fresh scallops with plump brightly coloured corals.

If good fish stock (home-made or Fonds de Cuisine, see page 34) is difficult to come by, use water with a little extra sea salt and a dash of wine.

3 HEADS OF BELGIAN CHICORY
1 ORANGE
50G/2OZ BUTTER
50ML/3 TBSP FISH STOCK
6-8 SCALLOPS, PREFERABLY
    WITH CORAL
2 TBSP NOILLY PRAT OR DRY
    VERMOUTH
SEA SALT AND FRESHLY GROUND
    BLACK PEPPER

1 Shred, rinse and pat dry the chicory.

2 Zest and juice the orange.

3 Melt half the butter in a wok, add the chicory and sweat it for 1-2 minutes.

4 Pour in the orange juice and fish stock.

5 Slice each scallop across horizontally into two discs. Put them on top of the chicory with the orange zest.

6 Cover the pan tightly and steam-boil for 2-3 minutes.

7 Using a slotted spoon, remove the scallops and chicory from the wok, put on a warmed plate, season to taste and keep warm.

8 Pour in the Noilly Prat or vermouth, turn up the heat and reduce the sauce for 1 minute.

9 Cut the rest of the butter into small pieces and whisk them into the sauce. Season and pour the finished sauce over the scallops.

KING PRAWNS WITH CORIANDER

4 KING PRAWNS IN THEIR
   SHELLS
PIECE OF FRESH GINGER,
   ABOUT 1CM/½IN ACROSS
1 GARLIC CLOVE
1 TSP GROUND CORIANDER
1 TSP PAPRIKA
1 TSP GROUND CUMIN
PINCH OF CAYENNE
3 TBSP WATER
1 TBSP VINEGAR
JUICE OF ½ LEMON
2 TBSP SUNFLOWER OIL

1   Rinse the unshelled prawns
and pat them dry, then trim off
their heads and feet.

2   Peel the ginger and garlic.

3   Whizz them in the food
processor with the coriander,
paprika, cumin and cayenne.

4   Add the water, vinegar, lemon
juice and half the oil. Whizz again
until smooth.

5   Heat the rest of the oil in a
wok.

6   Add the spice mixture and stir-
fry for 2-3 minutes over a
moderate heat.

7   Add the prawns and stir-fry for
2 minutes.

FILLETS OF SOLE WITH ORANGE

●

*Although most people automatically
buy Dover sole, we like the smaller
dabs, slip or lemon soles. Not only
are they much better value, but
they are also just the right size for
10-minute cooking. We usually
allow 170g/6oz fillets per person
and get our fishmonger to trim the
fish for us.*

*If very small cook whole, but
allow 1-2 minutes longer.*

1 LEMON
2 ORANGES
100ML/4FLOZ WHITE WINE
100ML/4FLOZ WATER
8 FILLETS OF SOLE
75ML/4 TBSP DOUBLE CREAM
BUNCH OF PARSLEY
SEA SALT AND FRESHLY GROUND
   BLACK PEPPER

1   Zest the lemon and juice both
oranges and the lemon.

2   In a saucepan, bring to the boil
the fruit juices, wine, water and
some sea salt. Reduce the heat and
leave to simmer gently.

3   Cut the fillets of sole into 2-4
strips lengthwise, depending on
size.

4   Add the strips of sole to the
pan and poach for 1-2 minutes,
until just stiffened.

5   Using a slotted spoon, remove
the sole from the pan. Put the
fillets on a warmed plate and keep
warm.

6   Turn up the heat and whisk the
liquid until it is reduced by one
third.

7   Reduce the heat to low and stir
in the cream and lemon zest.

8   Snip over the parsley, season
and pour the sauce over the sole.

*Top: King Prawns with Coriander;
Bottom: Grilled monkfish with Fennel
and Sun-dried Tomato Sauce (page 87)*

TROUT WITH LETTUCE

●

In spite of repeated pleas, even our friendliest of fishmongers draws the line at filleting trout. This means that there is no way that we can cook the fish in 10 minutes. Rather than leave it out altogether, however, we have included this favourite recipe on the grounds that the preparation time is minimal, even if the baking time does run to 20 minutes.

If time is not critical for this dish, excellent results are obtained by cooking the fish en papillote, *ie wrapped in a parcel of greaseproof paper or foil. The baking time then, however, should be about 20-25 minutes.*

½ CUCUMBER
2 COS LETTUCES
115G/4OZ SORREL LEAVES
3 SPRING ONIONS
SMALL BUNCH OF PARSLEY
1 TSP CORIANDER SEEDS
50G/2OZ BUTTER
4 SMALL TROUT, GUTTED
175ML/6FLOZ WHITE WINE
1 LEMON
SEA SALT AND FRESHLY GROUND
    BLACK PEPPER

1　Heat the oven to 190C/375F/ gas5. Bring a kettle to the boil.

2　Peel the cucumber and wash the vegetables.

3　Blanch 8 lettuce leaves in the boiling water for 1 minute. Drain and pat dry.

4　In the food processor whizz the rest of the lettuce with the sorrel, spring onions, cucumber, parsley and coriander seeds and seasoning to taste.

5　Use half the butter to grease a baking dish. Tip the mixture into the dish and spread it evenly over the base.

6　Season the insides of the trout and then wrap each with 2 of the blanched lettuce leaves.

7　Put the trout on top of the vegetable mixture. Pour over the white wine.

8　Juice the lemon and pour this over the trout, then dot with the remaining butter. Bake for 15-20 minutes, depending on size.

9　With a fish slice, transfer the fish to a dish. Season the vegetable mixture and spoon it over the trout.

FAST FISH SAUCES

As the simplest and fastest way of cooking fish is to grill, poach or fry it plainly, we like to prepare a fast sauce to go with it.

HOLLANDAISE SAUCES

Yes, you can make an excellent Hollandaise sauce in under 10 minutes! You must, however, have a food processor. Our Hollandaise sauces, and the Mousseline in particular, are well suited to the delicate texture and flavour of poached white fish.

1 BASIC HOLLANDAISE

In a small saucepan, boil 1 tablespoon of white wine vinegar and 4 tablespoons of water to reduce to about 1 tablespoon. Process 2 egg yolks until smooth, add the vinegar and whizz again briefly. Melt 140g/5oz unsalted butter and trickle this into the mixture with the machine running. Process until the sauce thickens, then season to taste with salt and freshly ground black pepper.

2 TARRAGON HOLLANDAISE

Into a small saucepan, snip a handful of fresh tarragon leaves. Add 1 tablespoon of white wine vinegar and 4 tablespoons of water and reduce. Continue as for Basic Hollandaise as above.

3 TOMATO HOLLANDAISE

In a food processor, whizz a tomato and pour this into a cup. Rinse the bowl and make the Basic Hollandaise as above. Add the tomato purée to the sauce before final seasoning and whizz briefly to mix it in.

4 ORANGE HOLLANDAISE

Juice a blood orange. Make the Basic Hollandaise as above. Then, with the food processor running, trickle in the orange juice. Season to taste.

5 MOUSSELINE HOLLANDAISE

Whisk 75ml/4 tbsp whipping cream to just about soft peak. Make the Basic Hollandaise as above, then fold in the cream to the finished sauce and season to taste.

BEURRE BLANC SAUCES

These classic sauces are surprisingly fast and simple. They suit most poached, grilled, or plainly baked fish.

1 BASIC BEURRE BLANC

In the food processor, whizz 2 shallots. In a small saucepan, simmer 150ml/¼pt white wine with the chopped shallots until the mixture is soft and syrupy. Remove from the heat. Cut 115g/4oz unsalted butter into small pieces and whisk them into the pan, one piece at a time, until the sauce is smooth and shiny. Season lightly with sea salt and freshly ground black pepper.

2 BEURRE BLANC WITH ANCHOVY

In the food processor, whizz 2 shallots with 2 drained anchovy fillets. Make the Basic Beurre Blanc as above, using the shallot and anchovy mixture. Season lightly with freshly ground black pepper only.

3 BEURRE BLANC WITH MUSTARD

Make a Basic Beurre Blanc as above, but whisk in 1 tablespoon of mustard before adding the pieces of butter. Snip in a handful of fresh parsley. Season lightly.

CREAM SAUCES

As with all our other recipes for quick reduced sauces, remember to use a wide pan so that the liquid evaporates quickly.

1 SAFFRON CREAM SAUCE

Pour 4 tablespoons of white wine into a saucepan. Snip in a few strands of saffron. Simmer to reduce by about half. Stir in 200ml/7floz single cream. Simmer, whisking occasionally, to reduce by about one-third. Beat in a knob of butter and season lightly with sea salt and freshly ground black pepper.

2 BASIL CREAM SAUCE

Pour 4 tablespoons of white wine into a saucepan. Simmer to reduce by about half. Stir in 200ml/7floz single cream. Simmer, whisking occasionally, to reduce by about one-third. In the food processor, whizz a handful of fresh basil leaves to shred finely and beat them into the sauce with a knob of butter. Season lightly with sea salt and freshly ground black pepper.

3 CUCUMBER CREAM SAUCE

In the food processor, whizz a small peeled and deseeded cucumber with a handful of fresh tarragon leaves. Melt a knob of butter in a saucepan and sweat the cucumber for 1-2 minutes. Add 5 tablespoons of white wine and simmer until syrupy. Stir in 250ml/8floz single cream. Simmer very gently, whisking occasionally, to reduce the sauce a little. Beat in a knob of butter and season with sea salt and freshly ground black pepper.

SAVOURY BUTTERS

Our no-cook butters should be made with unsalted butter as salted butter masks the taste and can spoil the delicate balance of flavour in a dish.

We serve these sauces to accompany firm-fleshed grilled fish. As a general rule the more robust the fish, the stronger flavour of butter it can take.

If you have the time, make a savoury butter in advance, roll it into a sausage shape in a sheet of greaseproof paper and chill for easy slicing into discs: otherwise, just paint or spread straight on the cooked fish.

These recipes are for 4 portions.

1 HERB BUTTER

In the food processor, whizz until smooth 50g/2oz of butter with a few leaves of parsley, chives, chervil and tarragon. Season with a little freshly ground black pepper.

2 ORANGE AND LEMON BUTTER

In the food processor, whizz a wedge each of a roughly chopped unpeeled orange and lemon to a purée. With the machine still running, add 50g/2oz of butter then season with a little freshly ground black pepper.

3 WATERCRESS BUTTER

In the food processor, whizz until smooth a handful of watercress with 50g/2oz of butter and a small pinch of sea salt.

4 GREEN PEPPERCORN BUTTER

In the food processor, whizz until smooth 2 teaspoons of drained green peppercorns with 50g/2oz of butter and a small pinch of sea salt.

5 DILL AND HORSERADISH BUTTER

In the food processor, whizz until smooth 50g/2oz of butter with a handful of fresh dill, 2 teaspoons of creamed horseradish and a little freshly ground black pepper.

6 MINT BUTTER

In the food processor, whizz until smooth 50g/2oz of butter with a handful of fresh mint leaves and a little sea salt and freshly ground black pepper.

7 SMOKED SALMON BUTTER

In the food processor, whizz until smooth 75g/3oz of butter with 25g/1oz smoked salmon trimmings, 1 or 2 tablespoons of lemon juice and a little freshly ground black pepper.

8 SHRIMP BUTTER

In the food processor, whizz until smooth 75g/3oz of butter with 25g/1oz well-drained peeled shrimp, 1 teaspoon of anchovy essence and a pinch of cayenne pepper.

9 VERMOUTH BUTTER

In the food processor, whizz until smooth 75g/3oz butter with a dash of dry vermouth and a little sea salt and freshly ground black pepper.

10 PERNOD BUTTER

In the food processor, whizz until smooth 75g/3oz of butter with a dash of Pernod, a pinch of fennel seeds and a little sea salt and freshly ground black pepper.

11 LIME BUTTER

In the food processor, whizz a coarsely chopped ½ lime to a purée. With the machine still running, add 75g/3oz butter and sea salt and freshly ground black pepper. Whizz until smooth.

12 CORIANDER BUTTER

In the food processor, whizz a handful of coriander seeds. With the machine still running, add 75g/3oz butter and sea salt and freshly ground black pepper. Whizz until smooth.

OLIVE OIL SAUCES

The quality of the olive oil is obviously critical here, and we only ever use extra-virgin. As these sauces are rather gutsy, they go best with strong-flavoured fish.

1 PARSLEY AND GARLIC SAUCE

In the food processor, whizz a handful of flat-leaf parsley, 1 garlic clove and the juice of 1 lemon with a pinch each of sea salt and cayenne pepper. With the machine running, trickle in 100ml/4floz olive oil. Process until thick and smooth.

2 FENNEL AND SUN-DRIED TOMATO SAUCE

In the food processor, coarsely shred ½ a fennel bulb. Blanch for 1 minute in boiling water then drain. Warm 100ml/4floz olive oil, add the fennel and snip in 2 sun-dried tomatoes. Season with sea salt and freshly ground black pepper and stir well.

3 AVOCADO AND OLIVE SAUCE

In the food processor, process until smooth 1 peeled avocado with 2 garlic cloves, 6 stoned black olives, a dash of Tabasco, the juice of ½ a lemon and 3 tablespoons of red wine. Warm 150ml/¼pt olive oil and stir in the mixture. Beat 1 egg yolk in a bowl and slowly whisk it into the warm mixture. Season with sea salt and freshly ground black pepper.

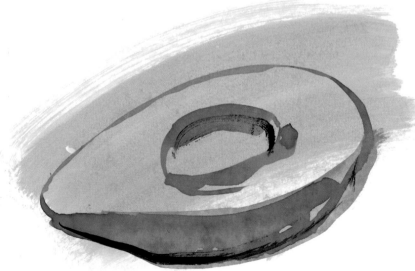

Meat and Poultry

In 10-minute cuisine, when it comes to meat and poultry we always opt for quality rather than quantity. The fact is that the more expensive cuts are the most tender. They are also usually well trimmed, they will need little preparation and they will generally cook a great deal faster.

The most suitable 10-minute techniques for cooking meat and poultry are pan-frying, stir-frying and grilling. The cooking method is dictated by the dish and the cut involved. For our purposes, pieces of meat and poultry should generally be no thinner than 0.5cm/¼in and no thicker than 2cm/¾in.

We tend to eat meat on the rare side – beef and lamb, in particular, we like pinkish. If you prefer your meat well done, you will obviously have to cook it slightly longer than the times we have given below.

Noisettes of Lamb with Tomatoes (page 97)

POUSSIN WITH HERBS AND OLIVES

●

When buying poussins, ask the butcher to spatchcock them: he will cut them along the backbone, then open them up and flatten them. The flatter the spatchcocked poussin, the quicker it will cook: so, before paste-painting, flatten them still further using the heel of the hand or a rolling pin.

The flesh of the poussins is also scored deeply with a sharp knife to speed up the cooking process and allow the flavours of the paste to permeate the poussin.

To tell when the poussins are cooked through, pierce the thickest piece of flesh with the tip of the sharp knife – the juices should run clear.

8 GARLIC CLOVES
14 STONED BLACK OLIVES
2 TBSP GROUND ALMONDS
HANDFUL EACH: THYME,
  MARJORAM, OREGANO AND
  FLAT-LEAF PARSLEY
5 TBSP OLIVE OIL
SEA SALT AND FRESHLY GROUND
  BLACK PEPPER
2 POUSSINS

1   Heat the grill until very hot.

2   In the food processor, whizz the garlic with the olives, almonds and herbs.

3   Add the olive oil, season generously and whizz again briefly to blend.

4   Using a sharp knife, deeply score the flesh of the poussins across several times.

5   Paste-paint the poussins all over with the prepared mixture.

6   Grill the poussins, turning them frequently, for 8-10 minutes until brown and cooked through. Cut in half to serve.

CHICKEN WINGS WITH MARMALADE

◑

2 SPRING ONIONS
4 TBSP MARMALADE
2 TBSP OLIVE OIL
½ LEMON
8 CHICKEN WINGS
SEA SALT AND FRESHLY GROUND
  BLACK PEPPER

1   Heat the grill until very hot.

2   In the food processor, whizz the spring onions and then add the marmalade and oil. Whizz again to blend well.

3   Juice the lemon and add the juice to the mixture. Season the mixture and whizz again briefly.

4   Paste-paint the chicken wings with the prepared mixture.

5   Grill the chicken wings for 6-8 minutes, turning them occasionally.

90

CHICKEN BREASTS WITH COURGETTES AND TARRAGON

●

3 COURGETTES
FEW SPRIGS OF TARRAGON
200ML/7FLOZ CHICKEN STOCK
1 TBSP WHITE WINE VINEGAR
4 BONED CHICKEN BREASTS
50G/2OZ BUTTER
SEA SALT AND FRESHLY GROUND
  BLACK PEPPER

1   Roughly slice the courgettes and spread them evenly in a sauté pan. Sprinkle them with half the tarragon leaves.

2   Pour in the chicken stock and vinegar. Cover the pan and steam-boil the courgettes over a moderate heat for a couple of minutes.

3   Meanwhile, skin the chicken breasts and cut each in half lengthwise.

4   Place the chicken pieces over the courgettes, sprinkle with sea salt and the remaining tarragon leaves.

5   Cover and steam-boil for 5 minutes.

6   Remove the chicken and courgettes from the pan, put them on a warmed plate and keep warm.

7   Turn up the heat under the pan and whisk the butter into the cooking liquid. Season this sauce and pour it over the chicken.

CHICKEN WITH VERMOUTH AND SAGE

●

4 BONED CHICKEN BREASTS
10 SAGE LEAVES
8 THIN SLICES OF PROSCIUTTO
1 TBSP OLIVE OIL
25G/1OZ BUTTER
100ML/4FLOZ DRY VERMOUTH
75ML/4TBSP SINGLE CREAM
SEA SALT AND FRESHLY GROUND
  BLACK PEPPER

1   Skin the chicken breasts and cut each in half lengthwise.

2   Snip a couple of sage leaves over each piece of breast.

3   Wrap each breast in 2 slices of the prosciutto. If necessary, secure the parcels with a wooden toothpick.

4   Heat the oil with the butter in a sauté pan over a moderate heat.

5   Sauté the parcels for 3-4 minutes on each side.

6   Pour in the vermouth and reduce the heat a little. Cover and cook for a further 2-3 minutes.

7   Remove the chicken from the pan, place on a warmed dish and keep warm.

8   Snip in the rest of sage and stir in the cream until heated through. Season the sauce and pour it over the chicken.

DUCK WITH CRANBERRY SAUCE

●

Boned duck breasts are now sold in most supermarkets. French 'magrets' tend to weigh approximately 350g/12oz and to be nearly twice the size of the average English duck breast. If you buy magrets, start off by cutting each diagonally across in half to end up with two 170g/6oz portions. To speed up the cooking of either, using a very sharp knife, make 4 or 5 deep slanting cuts through the skin and into the flesh.

If fresh cranberries are not available, use frozen ones instead and they will simply defrost as they are cooked.

125G/4OZ CRANBERRIES
2 TBSP SUGAR
2 TSP OLIVE OIL
4 ENGLISH DUCK BREASTS OR 2
   LARGE MAGRETS
75ML/4 TBSP PORT
SEA SALT AND FRESHLY GROUND
   BLACK PEPPER

1   Put the cranberries, sugar and water to cover in a small saucepan.

2   Bring to the boil, reduce the heat and simmer until the cranberries pop.

3   Heat the oil in a sauté pan.

4   If using magrets, cut each in half lengthwise. Slit the skin and flesh (see above) and season.

5   Sauté the duck – skin side down – for 3-4 minutes. Turn the duck over and sauté for a further 2-3 minutes. Occasionally press the pieces of duck down into the pan.

6   Using a slotted spoon, remove the duck from the pan, arrange on a warmed plate and keep warm.

7   Tip out most of the fat from the pan.

8   Turn up the heat. Pour the port into the pan and scrape the pan with a wooden spoon to deglaze, until most of the alcohol has been driven off.

9   Stir in the cranberries, season the sauce and pour it over the duck.

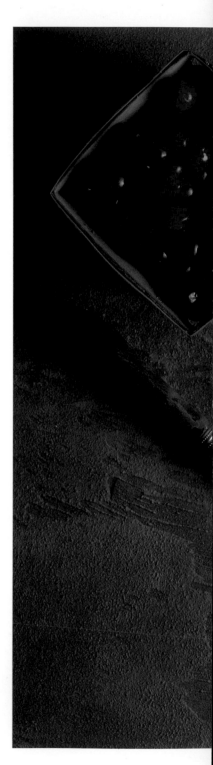

BLACK PUDDING WITH APPLE

●

Some butchers still make their own black puddings and these are usually worth buying. Otherwise, look out for fresh black puddings rather than the pre-packed varieties. Cut them into slices about 1cm/½in thick, which will cook fast without collapsing.

As for the apples, we prefer to use sweet dessert apples – such as Cox's or russets – as they cook fast, hold their shape well and have a good depth of flavour.

45G/1½OZ BUTTER

2 APPLES

450G/1LB BLACK PUDDING

100ML/4FLOZ DRY CIDER

2 TSP MUSTARD

SEA SALT AND FRESHLY GROUND
    BLACK PEPPER

1   Melt two-thirds of the butter in a frying pan.

2   Core the apples and then cut them into 8 slices.

3   Add the apples to the pan and fry them over a low heat, turning once.

4   Slice the black pudding (see above).

5   Push the apples to the side of the pan and add the black pudding.

6   Fry the black pudding over a low heat for 3-4 minutes on each side.

7   Using a slotted spoon, remove the black pudding and apple from the pan, arrange them on a warmed plate and keep warm.

8   Turn up the heat under the pan and pour in the cider.

9   Whisk in the rest of the butter along with the mustard. Scrape the pan well with a wooden spoon to deglaze. Season the sauce and pour it over the black pudding.

Left: Chicken with Vermouth and Sage (page 91) on a bed of rice; Right: Black Pudding with Apple.

CALF'S LIVER WITH RAISINS

●

No matter how thin the butcher usually slices calf's liver, ask him to slice it even thinner (ideally, it should be paper-thin) and allow about 140g/5oz per person. Use a large frying pan and cook the liver very fast so that it is seared on the outside but still remains pink inside.

1 TBSP RED WINE VINEGAR
1 TBSP WATER
1 TSP SUGAR
25G/1OZ RAISINS
4 SAGE LEAVES
45G/1½OZ BUTTER
4 SLICES CALF'S LIVER
SEA SALT AND FRESHLY GROUND
  BLACK PEPPER

1   Heat the vinegar, water, sugar, raisins and 2 sage leaves in a small saucepan until the liquid is boiling.

2   Reduce the heat and simmer for 1 minute, then season.

3   Melt the butter with the rest of the sage in a large frying pan. Add the liver and sauté over a moderate-to-high heat for 1 minute on each side.

4   Quickly remove the liver from the pan, put it on a warmed plate, season and keep warm.

5   Pour the vinegar mixture into the pan and turn up the heat a little.

6   Using a wooden spoon, scrape the pan to deglaze and drive off most of the vinegar. Pour the sauce over the liver.

CHICKEN LIVERS WITH ORANGE

◑

For this dish, we prefer to use a slightly sweet sherry – amontillado or, better still, oloroso. Both combine well with the orange.

225G/8OZ CHICKEN LIVERS
1 GARLIC CLOVE
½ ORANGE
1 TBSP OLIVE OIL
25G/1OZ BUTTER
2 TBSP SHERRY
FEW SPRIGS OF MARJORAM
SEA SALT AND FRESHLY GROUND
  BLACK PEPPER

1   Trim and slice the chicken livers. Rinse and pat them dry.

2   Chop the garlic.

3   Zest and juice the orange.

4   Heat the oil and butter in a sauté pan. Add the livers and garlic and sauté them for a few minutes – the exact timing will depend on how pink the livers are to be – turning from time to time.

5   Add the sherry, orange zest and juice and snip in the marjoram.

6   Season and stir for 1 minute before serving.

NOISETTES OF LAMB WITH TOMATOES

●

If you cannot find small noisettes of lamb weighing 50-75g/2-3oz (and no more than about 2cm/¾in thick), use lamb steaks instead (trimming off all their visible fat and cooking them 1 or 2 minutes longer).

The more fresh herbs used, the more pungent the sauce. If you are not entirely sure about the sweetness of the tomatoes, add a pinch of sugar.

3 RIPE TOMATOES
2 GARLIC CLOVES
FEW SPRIGS EACH OF:
   OREGANO, THYME, MARJORAM
   AND ROSEMARY
2 TBSP OLIVE OIL
8 NOISETTES OF LAMB
3 TBSP WHITE WINE
SEA SALT AND FRESHLY GROUND
   BLACK PEPPER
1 LEMON, TO SERVE

1 Whizz the tomatoes with the garlic and herbs.

2 Heat the oil in a sauté pan. Add 2 tablespoons of the prepared mixture and cook over a moderate heat for a minute or so.

3 Turn up the heat to high, season the noisettes and put them in the pan on top of the mixture. Cook them for 2-3 minutes on each side.

4 Remove the noisettes from the pan and put aside to keep warm

5 Add the remaining mixture to the pan, reduce the heat to moderate and cook for a minute or two.

6 Add the wine and stir for 1 minute.

7 Cut the lemon into quarters and serve to accompany the meat dressed with the pan juices.

CUTLETS OF LAMB WITH GINGER

●

Although expensive, best end of neck cutlets of lamb are lean, tender and cook very fast. As they tend to be rather small, we suggest 2 cutlets per person.

A low-fat yoghurt, unless slowly stirred into the sauce, is likely to curdle: so use a full-fat thick yoghurt, preferably made from sheep's milk.

PIECE OF FRESH GINGER,
   2.5CM/1IN ACROSS
1 GARLIC CLOVE
2 SPRING ONIONS
1 SPRIG OF FRESH LEMON
   GRASS
1 TBSP CHILLI OIL (SEE PAGE
   19)
8 LAMB CUTLETS
75ML/4 TBSP WHITE WINE
75ML/4 TBSP THICK YOGHURT
SEA SALT AND FRESHLY GROUND
   BLACK PEPPER

1 In the food processor, whizz the ginger with the garlic, spring onion, lemon grass, sea salt to taste and half of the chilli oil.

2 Paste-paint the lamb cutlets with the prepared mixture.

3 Heat the rest of the chilli oil in a sauté pan. Add the cutlets to the pan and sauté them for 3 minutes on each side.

4 Remove the meat from the pan, put on a warmed dish and keep warm.

5 Pour the wine and yoghurt into the pan and stir over a low heat for 1 minute.

6 Season the sauce and the lamb lightly, then pour the sauce over the meat.

STRIPS

Fillets and the more tender cuts of beef, veal, pork and chicken cook very fast indeed when cut into thin strips. Start off with slices about 0.5cm/¼in thick, then cut them across (preferably along the grain, for minimum shrinkage and maximum texture) into pieces about 5-7.5cm/2-3in long and 2.5cm/1in wide. A wok – with its deep sides and rounded base – is the ideal pan for cooking such strips. Make sure the cooking medium is hot enough to seize and seal the meat as soon as it hits the pan.

1 CHICKEN STRIPS WITH SESAME SEEDS

Cut 450g/1lb of boned and skinned chicken breasts into strips. Heat 1 tablespoon of oil in a wok. Stir-fry a handful of sesame seeds with 1-2 snipped spring onions for 1 minute. Add the chicken strips and stir-fry for 1-2 minutes. Stir in 1 tablespoon of soy sauce and a few drops of chilli sauce. Snip in a few leaves of fresh coriander and sprinkle in a dash of sesame oil. Season with sea salt and freshly ground black pepper and serve.

2 VEAL STRIPS WITH LEMON

Cut 450g/1lb of veal escalopes into strips. Heat about 100ml/4floz of a light (veal, chicken or vegetable) stock in a wok. Poach the veal gently in the stock along with a handful of tarragon leaves, a few green peppercorns and the zest of a lemon for a couple of minutes. Using a slotted spoon, remove the veal from the pan. Turn up the heat to reduce the stock a little. Add 3 tablespoons of thick yoghurt, a dash of lemon juice and a pinch of sugar. Tip the veal strips back in, stir together, season with sea salt and freshly ground black pepper and serve.

3 PORK STRIPS WITH SHIITAKE MUSHROOMS

Cut 450g/1lb of fillet of pork into strips. Heat 2 tablespoons of oil in a wok. Stir-fry the pork with a crushed garlic clove and a little chopped fresh ginger. Slice a ½ handful of shiitake mushrooms and add them to the wok with some mange-tout peas and 1 tablespoon of plum sauce. Stir-fry for a couple of minutes, sprinkle in a dash of dry sherry, season with sea salt and freshly ground black pepper and serve.

4 10-MINUTE STROGANOFF

Cut 450g/1lb of fillet steak into strips and sprinkle them generously with paprika. Heat 1 tablespoon of oil and a knob of butter in a wok over a high heat. Stir-fry the beef along with a couple of snipped spring onions for a couple of minutes and remove with a slotted spoon. Pour out the oil. Over a low heat, swirl in 1-2 tablespoons of brandy, 1 teaspoon of tomato ketchup, a dash of lemon juice and a small (150ml/¼pt) carton of sour cream. Simmer for a minute or two, tip the beef strips back in and stir together. Season with sea salt and freshly ground black pepper and serve.

10-minute Stroganoff with Basic Butter Noodles (page 106)

10-MINUTE HAMBURGERS

Even before the recent worries about the wisdom of eating beef, we never bought ready-made mince, preferring to whizz our own from lean steak. When doing this, be very careful not to over-process as this ruins the texture and makes the mince far too heavy and dense.

The ideal weight for fast-cooking burgers is about 70g/2½oz and the fastest way to shape them is to take roughly the right amount of mince between the palms of the hands, roll it into a round ball and then flatten this into a pattie. The fastest means of cooking hamburgers is either to grill or pan-fry them, making sure that the grill or frying pan is thoroughly heated beforehand. Allow 2 per person.

1 BASIC HAMBURGER

Whizz 285g/10oz trimmed and roughly chopped steak with 1 spring onion, 1 egg, 1 teaspoon of mustard, and a dash each of tomato purée, Worcestershire sauce and Tabasco. Season well with sea salt and freshly ground black pepper. Make into 4 patties.

2 SPICED HAMBURGER

Whizz 285g/10oz trimmed and roughly chopped steak with 1-2 spring onions, 2 teaspoons of harissa (or chilli sauce) and a pinch each of ground cumin, coriander and cinnamon. Season with sea salt and freshly ground black pepper.

3 HERB HAMBURGER

Whizz 285g/10oz trimmed and roughly chopped steak with 1 garlic clove, 1 teaspoon of mustard and a handful each of: parsley, summer savory, thyme and rosemary. Season with sea salt and freshly ground black pepper.

4 CHILLI HAMBURGER

Whizz 285g/10oz trimmed and roughly chopped steak with a garlic clove, 1 teaspoon each of chilli and soy sauce and a dash of anchovy essence. Season with sea salt and freshly ground black pepper.

GRILLED MEAT & POULTRY

The most obvious and simplest way of cooking meat and poultry fast is to grill it. For this treatment it is particularly important to buy top-quality produce. Despite their size, whole pieces of meat actually cook just as fast as kebabs, which are fiddly and time-consuming to skewer on sticks.

We always choose well-hung, finely trimmed cuts with the minimum of visible fat. Unfortunately, these types of cut – fillets, tenderloins, best end and noisettes, for example – are the most expensive. Pieces of meat and poultry for grilling should be about 1-2cm/½-¾in thick, and we usually allow about 115-170g/4-6oz per person. Grilled meat and poultry are best either paste-painted before grilling or served with a savoury butter (see below).

PASTE-PAINTS

As we have already mentioned on page 31, paste-painting is 10-minute cuisine's answer to marinating. As the meat or poultry grills, the paste holds in the flavour and creates a crust which adds extra taste and texture.

Most of these mixtures may also be served as side-sauces to accompany plainly grilled meat and poultry.

1 CORIANDER AND CUMIN

Mix 1 teaspoon each of ground coriander and cumin with a dash of harissa (or chilli sauce), the juice of 1 lime, sea salt and freshly ground black pepper and 4 tablespoons of thick yoghurt. Good with lamb.

2 YOGHURT AND MINT

In the food processor, whizz 4 tablespoons of thick yoghurt with a handful of mint leaves, 1 garlic clove, a pinch each of ground turmeric, cumin and coriander and sea salt and freshly ground black pepper. Good with lamb or chicken.

3 HONEY AND MUSTARD

Mix together 1 tablespoon of runny honey with 1 tablespoon of coarse-grain mustard, 2 teaspoons of tomato purée and 2 tablespoons of olive oil. Season lightly with sea salt and freshly ground black pepper. Good with all poultry.

4 ORANGE AND PORT

In the food processor, whizz $\frac{1}{4}$ of a roughly chopped unpeeled orange to a purée. Whizz in a handful of thyme and parsley and 2 teaspoons each of port, redcurrant jelly and olive oil. Good with venison.

5 BLUE CHEESE

Whizz 75g/3oz blue cheese with a garlic clove, 2 teaspoons of brandy and 1 tablespoon of olive oil until smooth. Season with freshly ground black pepper. Good with steaks.

SAVOURY BUTTERS

Make these with unsalted butter, and see page 86 for the fast and simple technique for preparing them.

1 ORANGE AND HERB BUTTER

In the food processor, whizz a wedge of a roughly chopped unpeeled orange to a purée. With the machine still running, add 50g/2oz of butter, 1-2 sage leaves and several sprigs each of rosemary, chives and parsley. Season with sea salt and freshly ground black pepper. Good with beef and chicken.

2 BRANDY AND PEPPER BUTTER

In the food processor, whizz until smooth 50g/2oz of butter with 1 tablespoon of brandy, a few black peppercorns, 1 teaspoon of mustard and a few leaves of parsley. Good with beef.

3 MUSHROOM BUTTER

In the food processor, whizz until smooth 50g/2oz butter with a few mushrooms, 1 spring onion, a dash of sherry and a pinch of cayenne. Good with beef and poultry.

4 SHALLOT AND TOMATO BUTTER

In the food processor, whizz until smooth 1 small ripe tomato with 2 shallots, a few sprigs of parsley, a dash of lemon juice and 50g/2oz butter. Season with sea salt and freshly ground black pepper. Good with steaks.

Vegetables, Noodles and Rice

In 10-minute cuisine there is really not a great deal of time for vegetables and other accompaniments – and, in any case, we always serve a salad!

For these reasons we keep our vegetables, rice and noodles relatively simple. Since there is often no time to prepare separate dishes, one good trick is to combine them and to cook vegetables along with rice or noodles.

Grilled vegetables (page 105)

VEGETABLES

It will come as no surprise to learn that here, as everywhere else, we use only fresh vegetables (the only possible exceptions are frozen spinach and tins of petits pois).

We have 3 basic techniques for cooking vegetables in 10 minutes:

Grilled chicken breast paste-painted with Honey and Mustard (page 101) and served with steam-boiled broccoli and mange-tout peas

STEAM-BOILING

As you would expect, this is a mixture of steaming and boiling and incorporates the best aspects of both techniques. As with steaming, the true taste, texture and most of the nutrients of the vegetables are maintained, but this is achieved with the speed of boiling.

The only equipment needed is a good wide-bottomed saucepan with a tight-fitting lid. Into this, put just enough lightly salted boiling water to cover the bottom. Then tip in the vegetables, cover and boil over a high heat for a couple of minutes (for crunchy vegetables) or until cooked as preferred. To check whether the vegetables are done, lift the lid and test for texture with the point of a sharp knife. Once cooked, drain the vegetables thoroughly and season.

Tiny baby vegetables, such as carrots, baby sweetcorn, courgettes, asparagus sprue, cherry tomatoes, mange-tout peas and French beans can be cooked whole. Otherwise, slice, chop, sliver or shred them. The ideal size varies with the vegetable.

Cauliflower and broccoli are best broken into tiny florets no larger than 2.5cm/1in. Larger carrots and courgettes, celery and leeks can either be cut into 2.5cm/1in slices or shredded (see page 30). Keep the tips of large, thick asparagus whole; the stems, like bobby and runner beans, cook faster when slivered (see page 30).

The quickest (if slightly wasteful) way of preparing French beans is to grab a handful, knock them on a work surface to align the tops, snip off those tops, turn them over, bang again to align the tails and snip these off. If the beans are still too long, snip them across in half.

GRILLING

Grilled vegetables are delicious – with robust textures and tastes – and their slightly burnt, charred flavour is a great joy.

To prepare them for grilling, slice vegetables in half lengthwise (and in half again, if they are very big!). Then paint them lightly all over with olive oil and sprinkle them with sea salt.

Heat the grill until very hot and cook the vegetables for a few minutes on each side until just soft and tender. Do not worry if they look slightly charred, it only improves their flavour.

Most Mediterranean vegetables are ideal for this treatment. Sadly, not all of them cook fast enough –

but the ones that suit our purposes include courgettes, sweet peppers, onions, fennel, chicories (including radicchio) and tomatoes.

SAUTÉING OR STIR-FRYING

What you call this method depends really on whether a wok or a sauté pan is being used. As with steam-boiling, all but the tiniest vegetables must be trimmed to a suitable size.

Whichever pan is being used, heat just enough oil, butter (butter on its own does tend to blacken and burn), or a mixture of both, to coat the bottom of the pan and tip in the prepared vegetables. Stir them over a moderate heat until they are cooked to taste – it probably will not be more than about 3 minutes – and season.

Whole button or sliced larger mushrooms, baby sweetcorn, mange-tout peas, peas, shredded spinach or lettuce leaves, slivered cucumbers or courgettes and bean sprouts are all quick to prepare and sauté or stir-fry well.

NOODLES

We eat noodles – both European and Oriental varieties – with most of our meat and fish dishes.

According to Yan-Kit So, the well-known Chinese food writer, there are over 500 types of Oriental noodle, all made with different ingredients or in various shapes.

For this reason, do not just rely on the small selection of noodles available in your local supermarket. Be adventurous – raid an Oriental specialist shop and stock up with as many kinds as appeal to you! Look out for cellophane, thread, bean curd, egg, wheat, rice-flour and shrimp and other flavoured noodles. As they are so cheap, if they don't go down well it will not have been an expensive mistake.

BASIC WAYS OF COOKING NOODLES

Always follow the instructions on the packet. Generally speaking, cellophane noodles are simply soaked in very hot water for a few minutes until soft. They are then drained and chopped to a manageable size.

For wheat or egg noodles, cook them in boiling salted water for 3-4 minutes until soft. Then drain, refresh, separate them and drain them again, if necessary.

Once cooked, noodles can be finished in different ways:

1 BASIC BUTTER NOODLES

Prepare the noodles as described on the previous page. Stir in a knob of butter. Season with sea salt and freshly ground black pepper.

2 BASIC OIL NOODLES

Prepare the noodles as above. Stir in 1 tablespoon of oil and season. The oil you use will depend on the main dish: for a strong flavour, add a few drops of sesame oil: for a milder flavour, plain groundnut or sunflower oil is preferable.

3 HERB NOODLES

Prepare the noodles as above, finishing with either butter or oil. Snip in a handful of chives, flat-leaf parsley or chervil.

TWICE-COOKED NOODLES

Twice-cooking is a traditional Chinese two-step technique, often involving first simmering then stir-frying. We use it to add flavour, interest and bite to plain noodles and most of the twice-cooked noodle dishes below, in sufficient quantity, make ideal 10-minute snacks or simple meals in themselves.

1 MUSHROOM NOODLES

In a wok, heat 1 tablespoon of olive oil. Add a few sliced oyster mushrooms and stir-fry for 1-2 minutes. Add the prepared noodles (see page 105) and stir-fry until heated through. Season with sea salt and freshly ground black pepper.

2 MANGE-TOUT NOODLES

In a wok, heat 1 tablespoon of olive oil. Snip in a spring onion and a handful of mange-tout peas. Stir-fry for 1-2 minutes. Add the prepared noodles (see above) and stir-fry until heated through. Season with sea salt and freshly ground black pepper.

Mange-tout Noodles

3 LEEK NOODLES

In a wok, heat 1 tablespoon of olive oil. Add 1 shredded leek and a pinch of thyme and stir-fry for 1-2 minutes. Add the prepared noodles (see above) and stir-fry until heated through. Season with sea salt and freshly ground black pepper.

4 SUN-DRIED TOMATO NOODLES

In a wok, heat 1 tablespoon of the oil from sun-dried tomatoes. Snip in a couple of sun-dried tomatoes (see page 18) and stir-fry for 1 minute. Add the prepared noodles (see above). Snip in a few basil leaves and stir-fry until heated through. Season with sea salt and freshly ground black pepper.

5 ALMOND NOODLES

In a wok, heat 1 tablespoon of olive oil. Add a handful of almond slivers and stir-fry for 1-2 minutes. Add the prepared noodles (see above) and stir-fry until heated through. Season with sea salt and freshly ground black pepper.

6 ROASTED GARLIC NOODLES

In a wok, heat 1 tablespoon of the oil from roasted garlic (see page 19). Add a couple of the roasted cloves, mash and stir-fry for 1-2 minutes. Add the prepared noodles (see above), snip in a handful of flat-leaf parsley and stir-fry until heated through. Season with sea salt and freshly ground black pepper.

7 CHILLI NOODLES 1

In a wok, heat 1 tablespoon of oil. Snip in a couple of spring onions and add a pinch of chilli powder. Add the prepared noodles (see above) and stir-fry for 1-2 minutes. Sprinkle over a few drops of soy sauce.

8 CHILLI NOODLES 2

In a wok, heat 1 tablespoon of oil. Add a couple of dried chillis and stir-fry for 2-3 minutes. Add the prepared noodles (see above) and stir-fry until heated through. Season.

VEGETABLES, NOODLES & RICE

RICE

Sadly, the more interesting varieties of rice (brown, basmati, arborio) have to be avoided by the 10-minute cook on the grounds that they take far too long.

What we have found, however, is that the partially cooked convenience packets of rice work very well, especially if flavoured with some of our Bits and Pieces for Rice (see below).

COOKING RICE

Always follow the instructions on the packet. Generally speaking, rice will taste much better if it is cooked in stock rather than water. This works better still if the stock complements the main dish: for example, if you are serving chicken and have either chicken or vegetable stock handy, use it to cook the rice.

BITS & PIECES
FOR RICE

1   Mix a couple of cinnamon sticks with the rice and boil them together.

2   Mix a couple of bay leaves with the rice and boil them together.

3   Mix a few sprigs of thyme with the rice and boil them together.

4   Mix a few dried wild mushrooms with the rice and boil them together.

5   While the rice is simmering, throw in a handful of pine kernels.

6   While the rice is simmering, add a few sliced mushrooms and a knob of butter.

7   While the rice is simmering, add a pinch of powdered saffron and a knob of butter.

8   While the rice is simmering, add a few sprigs of tarragon, a dash of white wine vinegar and a knob of butter.

9   Once the rice is cooked, stir in a knob of Orange and Lemon butter (see page 86).

10   Once the rice is cooked, stir in some grated Cheddar and a knob of butter.

11   Once the rice is cooked, snip in some chives and chervil and stir in a knob of butter.

12   Once the rice is cooked, stir in 1-2 tablespoons of olive oil and a dash of vinegar.

Last Courses

Fresh fruit is one of the easiest and most satisfying ways to finish off any meal: the other is a selection of good cheeses. However, some people feel very deprived without a proper pudding; so for all those with a sweet tooth we have happily concocted some 10-minute last courses.

Frosted fruit (page 112)

FRESH FRUIT

Use whatever fruits are in season, choosing for taste, colour and shape.

Most fruits look more appealing left on their stalks or with their leaves intact – particularly berries and citrus fruits.

Make a fuss of your fruit and, for a sumptuous show, arrange it as a table centrepiece on a dish or flat-sided bowl, piling the fruit high in a generous mound and letting some hang over the sides. Alternatively, just place them on the table amidst a bed of ivy or vine leaves.

In among the fruit, tuck: sprigs of mint and other edible leaves; miniature biscuits, such as florentines, amaretti and cantucci; sweets, such as slices of panforte, nougat, candied fruit and mint crisps; or even dried and crystallized fruit, such as figs, apricots, dates and prunes.

FROSTED FRUIT

SEASONAL FRUIT: SUCH AS
   STRAWBERRIES, GRAPES,
   REDCURRANTS, WHITE- OR
   BLACKCURRANTS,
   TANGERINES, APPLES ETC
LEMONS, AS REQUIRED
ICING SUGAR, AS REQUIRED

1   Wash the fruit and pat it dry.

2   If using larger fruit, cut it into bite-sized pieces and sprinkle with lemon juice.

3   Arrange the fruit on a plate (see above).

4   Sieve the icing sugar over it until it is all covered with a light film.

5   Chill the dusted fruit while the rest of the meal is in progress, and serve straight from the refrigerator.

PEACHES WITH AMARETTI

Look out for white peaches as they have an incredibly intense flavour. There is no need to peel them, simply wipe them clean. It is much quicker and cheaper to buy amaretti unwrapped in packets, rather than buying the individually wrapped type.

4 WHITE PEACHES
50G/2OZ AMARETTI BISCUITS
45G/1½OZ BUTTER

1   Heat the oven to 190C/375F/gas5.

2   Wash, pat dry, halve and stone the peaches. Arrange in a gratin dish.

3   In a food processor, whizz the biscuits to crumbs and scatter these over the peaches.

4   Dot the crumbs with butter and bake in the oven for 7 minutes.

5   Finish by browning the topping briefly under a very hot grill.

PAN-FRIED APPLE SLICES

We prefer to use dessert apples, such as Cox's or russets, as they cook faster, have a better sweeter flavour and retain their shape and texture.

4 DESSERT APPLES
50G/2OZ UNSALTED BUTTER
2 TBSP RAISINS IN WHISKY (SEE
   STORE-CUPBOARD SAUCES,
   PAGE 18)
2 TBSP SYRUP FROM THE
   RAISINS IN WHISKY (SEE
   ABOVE)
1 TBSP RUNNY HONEY
CRÈME FRAÎCHE OR THICK
   YOGHURT, TO SERVE

1   Wash, pat dry, quarter and core the apples. Cut each quarter again in half.

2   Melt the butter in a frying pan.

3   Add the apple slices and sauté them gently for 3-5 minutes.

4   Remove the apples from the pan with a slotted spoon and put on a warmed dish.

5   Pour the raisins and their syrup into the pan.

6   Stir in the honey and simmer for 1 minute.

7   Pour the mixture over the cooked apples. Serve with crème fraîche or thick yoghurt.

BAKED BANANAS

Overripe bananas will collapse into a mush, so use only firm fruit for this recipe.

4 BANANAS
6 TBSP APRICOT JAM
2 TBSP VODKA
SMALL HANDFUL OF MINT
    LEAVES
25G/1OZ UNSALTED BUTTER

1 Heat the oven to 220C/425F/gas 7.

2 Peel and split the bananas lengthwise.

3 Put each banana half on a piece of kitchen foil large enough to be able to wrap it generously.

4 In a small bowl, mix the apricot jam with the vodka and snip in the mint leaves.

5 Paste-paint each banana with the mixture, dot with butter and wrap the foil around the bananas to make individual parcels.

6 Bake the banana parcels for 10 minutes.

FRUIT GRATIN

This combination of plums and Mascarpone is our favourite fruit gratin. However, any fruit can be used, and Mascarpone can be replaced by double cream or crème fraîche.

8 PLUMS
75ML/4 TBSP MASCARPONE
4 TBSP GRANULATED SUGAR

1 Heat the grill.

2 Wash, pat dry, halve and stone the plums. Put in a gratin dish.

3 Dollop the mascarpone over the plums and sprinkle them with the sugar.

4 Grill until caramelized.

FRUIT SKEWERS

Most kebabs are a waste of time for the 10-minute cook, but these fruit skewers are worth a few precious moments. Use firm-textured fruit which will not collapse: whole strawberries and grapes; halved apricots, figs and plums; slices of pear and apple; segments of orange, grapefruit, clementine and mandarin, and chunks of pineapple.

Thread the prepared fruit on skewers. If you are leaving them while you prepare the first course, sprinkle them with lemon juice so that they do not discolour.

Just before grilling, paste-paint them with one of the sweet butters described on page 114. Grill for about 1 minute on each side, just enough to melt the butter and heat the fruit through.

SWEET BUTTERS

1 RUM BUTTER

In the food processor, whizz until smooth 50g/2oz unsalted butter with 1 tablespoon of rum and 1 tablespoon of brown sugar. Good with pineapple.

2 COINTREAU BUTTER

In the food processor, whizz until smooth 50g/2oz unsalted butter with 1 tablespoon of Cointreau and 1 tablespoon of icing sugar. Good with orange or grapefruit.

3 AMARETTO BUTTER

In the food processor, whizz 50g/2oz unsalted butter with 1 tablespoon amaretto liqueur and a couple of amaretti biscuits. Good with plums.

4 BRANDY BUTTER

In the food processor, whizz until smooth 50g/2oz unsalted butter with 2 tablespoons of brandy and 1 tablespoon of brown sugar. Good with apricots.

5 WHISKY BUTTER

In the food processor, whizz until smooth 50g/2oz unsalted butter with 1 tablespoon of whisky, a small piece of crystallized ginger and 1 tablespoon of icing sugar. Good with strawberries or oranges.

6 GIN BUTTER

In the food processor, whizz 50g/2oz unsalted butter with 1 tablespoon of gin, 1 tablespoon of icing sugar and a pinch of ground almonds. Good with plums.

FRUITS IN ALCOHOL

Fruit steeped in alcohol is an effortless – but impressive – last course. Use ripe fruit and carefully match it to the alcohol, then simply leave it to macerate while the meal is in progress.

1 PEACHES IN ROSÉ WINE

Cut 4 ripe peaches in half. Stone and cut them in half again. Put the prepared slices into 4 large wine glasses and pour over enough good Loire rosé to cover them. Chill.

2 STRAWBERRIES WITH KIRSCH

Wipe and hull 450g/1lb strawberries. Put them in a bowl and sprinkle with 2 tablespoons of Kirsch and a handful of mint leaves. Chill and serve with a bowl of thick set yoghurt beaten with icing sugar to taste.

3 STRAWBERRIES WITH COINTREAU

Wipe and hull 450g/1lb strawberries. Put them in a bowl and sprinkle with 2 tablespoons of Cointreau, along with the zest and juice of 1 orange. Chill.

4 MELON WITH MUSCAT

Halve and scoop out the seeds from 2 small melons. Cut a slice off the base of each half so that they lie flat, then pour into each 2-3 tablespoons of Muscat de Beaumes de Venise, Orange Muscat, or any heavily scented honeyed dessert wine. Chill.

5 GRAPES WITH KIRSCH

Mix together a generous 450g/1lb seedless grapes with a small carton (150ml/¼pt) of crème fraîche, a sprinkling of brown sugar and 3 tablespoons of Kirsch. Chill.

FRUIT FOOLS

Choose very ripe fruit and serve with amaretti biscuits, brandy snaps or any good tiny bought biscuit.

1 MANGO AND LIME FOOL

In a food processor, whizz 1 ripe peeled and chopped mango with $\frac{1}{4}$ of a fresh lime. Add 3 tablespoons of thick yoghurt and 1 tablespoon of double cream and whizz again briefly. Sweeten to taste with icing sugar.

2 RASPBERRY AND LEMON BALM FOOL

In a food processor, whizz 450g/ 1lb ripe raspberries with a handful of lemon balm leaves and a dash of Cassis. (If time allows, sieve the pips out at this stage.) Add 4 tablespoons of double cream and whizz again briefly. Sweeten to taste with icing sugar.

Raspberry and Lemon Balm Fool

LAST COURSES

ICE-CREAM

There is nothing wrong with using a bought ice-cream, provided it is a good one. We both like vanilla flavour and find that it works best with our sweet sauces.

ICE-CREAM SAUCES

1 HOT APRICOT SAUCE

Melt 25g/1oz of unsalted butter in a frying pan. Stir in a handful of chopped hazelnuts and brown briefly. Stir in 4 tablespoons of apricot jam and a dash of sweet wine. Simmer for a couple of minutes.

2 HOT MARMALADE SAUCE

In a saucepan, heat together 4 tablespoons of marmalade with 1 tablespoon of whisky until just bubbling.

3 WALNUT AND HONEY SAUCE

Melt 25g/1oz of unsalted butter in a frying pan. Stir in a handful of chopped walnuts and brown briefly. Add 2 tablespoons of runny honey and 2 tablespoons of whisky. Stir until heated through.

Vanilla ice-cream with Walnut and Honey Sauce

4 CHOCOLATE AND COFFEE SAUCE

Melt 25g/1oz of unsalted butter in a saucepan. Add 75g/3oz dark chocolate with 1 tablespoon of water and stir over a low heat until melted. Pour in 2 or 3 tablespoons of strong black coffee and 1 tablespoon of brandy. Sweeten to taste with a little icing sugar.

5 STORE-CUPBOARD SAUCES

Simply use either Raisins in Whisky or Prunes in Brandy (see page 19) spooned over the ice-cream.

Menu Suggestions

We have put together a range of menus which we hope will help the reader use the book to even greater effect. When planning these menus we obviously took into account a balance of tastes and textures, but we have also tried to make working in the kitchen as simple and as fast as possible. With this in mind, we have tried to ensure that the same cooking technique or piece of equipment is never used more than once in each menu.

For ease of reference, our menus are divided into four categories:

VERY FAST – where the whole meal may be cooked in *almost* 10 minutes

FORMAL – for very fast entertaining

INFORMAL – for very fast lunches and suppers

MEATLESS – for vegetarian and 'demi-veg' meals (containing some fish, but no meat or poultry)

VERY FAST

Avocado, Spinach and Lemon Soup (*page 36*)
Pasta with Raw Egg, Parma Ham and Chives (*page 45*)
Strawberries with Cointreau (*page 114*)

Pine Kernel Soup (*page 36*)
Pasta with Fresh Tomatoes and Mint (*page 45*)
Salad with Pour-over Dressing (*page 57*)
Fruit and cheese

Mushrooms, Shallot and Cream Eggs en Cocotte (*page 53*)
Chicken Livers with Orange (*page 96*)
Salad with Walnuts (*page 61*)
Fruit

Smoked Trout and Dill Eggs (*page 50*)
Salad with Avocado (*page 60*)
Fruit and cheese

Egg and Blue Cheese Salad (*page 67*)
Melon with Muscat (*page 114*)

FORMAL

Basic Eggs en Cocotte (*page 53*)
Noisettes of Lamb with Tomatoes (*page 97*)
Flageolets (*page 21*)
Fresh Fruit (*page 112*)

Five-spice Seared Salmon (*page 76*)
Mange-tout Noodles (*page 106*)
Salad with Avocado (*page 60*)
Peaches in Rosé Wine (*page 114*)

Sweetcorn Soup (*page 20*)
Chicken with Vermouth and Sage (*page 91*)
Rice with Pine Kernels (*page 109*)
Salad with Pour-over Dressing (*page 57*)
Cheese

Melon Salad (*page 62*)
Pan-fried Tuna with Anchovy and Capers (*page 75*)
Vanilla ice-cream with Chocolate and Coffee Sauce (*page 117*)

Chicken Wings with Marmalade (*page 90*)
Pasta with Fresh Tomatoes and Mint (*page 45*)
Salad with Anchovy Vinaigrette (*page 59*)
Peaches with Amaretti (*page 112*)

Watercress, Herb and Cream
Cheese Eggs en Cocotte (*page 53*)
Duck with Cranberry Sauce (*page 92*)
Rice with Bay Leaves (*page 109*)
Salad with Pour-over Dressing (*page 57*)
Fresh Fruit (*page 112*)

King Prawns with Coriander (*page 80*)
Grilled steaks with Brandy and
Pepper Butter (*page 101*)
Steam-boiled Vegetables (*page 104*)
Fruit Gratin (*page 113*)

Mushroom Salad (*page 68*)
Poussin with Herbs and Olives (*page 90*)
Mange-tout Noodles (*page 106*)
Raspberry and Lemon Balm Fool (*page 115*)

INFORMAL

Herb Velouté (*page 37*)
Black Pudding with Apple (*page 94*)
Ice-cream with Hot Marmalade
Sauce (*page 117*)

Herb Hamburger (*page 100*)
Grilled Vegetables (*page 105*)
Vanilla ice-cream with Walnut and
Honey Sauce (*page 117*)

Cauliflower Soup (*page 40*)
Chicken Liver and Chilli Salad (*page 62*)
Pan-fried Apple Slices (*page 112*)

Bean and Tuna Salad (*page 21*)
Ham and Leek Stir-fried Eggs (*page 50*)
Steam-boiled Vegetables (*page 104*)
Fresh Fruit (*page 112*)

Leek Salad (*page 64*)
10-minute Stroganoff (*page 98*)
Basic Butter Noodles (*page 106*)
Frosted Fruit (*page 112*)

MEATLESS

Carrot and Lime Juice Salad (*page 64*)
Pasta with Walnut and Thyme (*page 45*)
Salad with Black Olives (*page 60*)
Fruit Skewers with Rum Butter (*pages 113 and 114*)

Lettuce and Pea Soup (*page 37*)
Courgette, Tomato and Thyme
Eggah (*page 51*)
Salad with Parmesan (*page 61*)
Fresh Fruit (*page 112*)

Quick-marinated Smoked Haddock (*page 78*)
Pasta with Shredded Courgettes,
Pine Kernels and Tarragon (*page 47*)
Salad with Labna Balls (*page 18*)
Melon with Muscat (*page 114*)

Cucumber and Tarragon Soup (*page 36*)
Cod Steaks with Mustard (*page 78*)
Rice with Thyme (*page 109*)
Mango and Lime Fool (*page 115*)

Tomato Soup (*page 36*)
Grilled fish with Green Peppercorn
Butter (*page 86*)
Salad with Coriander and Parsley
Dressing (*page 59*)
Baked Bananas (*page 113*)

Tarator (*page 36*)
Pasta with Anchovies, Capers,
Parsley and Thyme (*page 45*)
Salad with Black Olives (*page 60*)
Strawberries with Kirsch (*page 114*)

MENU SUGGESTIONS

Index

For reasons of length, we have only been able to list occurrences of items as a principal ingredient.

Acknowledgments

The authors would like to express their thanks to:

Alaphia Bidwell, Anna del Conte, Peter Graham, Jack Lang, Heidi Lascelles, Patricia Lousada, Anne-Sophie Naudin, Sri Owen and Yan-Kit So for kindly contributing recipes or allowing us to quote from their recipes.

Anne Furniss, Lewis Esson, Paul Welti, Jess Koppel and Penny Mishcon for their help, encouragement and patience.

Finally to the members of the Cinema Club for their constructive (and, at times, destructive) criticism.

The publishers would also like to thank Magimix for their cooperation in lending one of their Système Cuisine food processors for use in photography.